Saints and Sandinistas

4·50

Saints and Sandinistas

The Catholic Church in Nicaragua and
its Response to the Revolution

Andrew Bradstock

EPWORTH PRESS

British Library Cataloguing in Publication Data

Bradstock, Andrew
    Saints and Sandinistas: the Catholic
    Church in Nicaragua and its response to
    the revolution.
    1. Catholic Church — Nicaragua 2. Church
    and State — Nicaragua 3. Nicaragua —
    Politics and government — 1979–
    I. Title
    972.85′053   F1528
    ISBN 0–7162–0432–0

First published in 1987
by Epworth Press
Room 195, 1 Central Buildings,
Westminster, London SW1

Typeset at The Spartan Press Ltd
Lymington, Hants
and printed in Great Britain by
Richard Clay Ltd, Bungay, Suffolk

Contents

You are the God of the poor
the human and simple God
the God that sweats in the street
the God with the weathered face
That's why I can talk to you
the way my own people talk
because you are the labourer God
the worker Christ
Hand in hand you walk with my people
you struggle in the fields and the city . . .

you have conquered death
and by your immense sacrifice
you have begotten the new human
who is destined for liberation
You live again
each time we raise an arm
to defend the people
from the dominion of exploitation
because you are alive on the farm
in the factory, in the school
I believe in your struggle without truce
I believe in your resurrection . . .

from the Nicaraguan Peasant Mass

Preface

In July 1979 the Sandinista National Liberation Front led a popular insurrection in Nicaragua, deposing President Anastasio Somoza Debayle and bringing to an end his family's forty-three year domination over the country. The revolution had several remarkable features, not the least of which was the degree of support it received from the Catholic church and individual priests, religious and lay-people. The aim of this book is to explore the origins, nature and extent of the church's involvement in the revolution, and the effect it has had both on the process itself and on the church's own role and mission. Three questions in particular will provide a focus for the discussion: what factors led church-people to participate in the process; what explanations might account for their divergent attitudes to the process both before and since the revolution; and what effect its divided response to the revolution has had on the Catholic church and the nature of religious belief in Nicaragua.

A great deal has been said and written about theologies of liberation, preferential options for the poor, and new structures for the church, but what is happening in Nicaragua enables us to move on to consider how these theologies, options and ecclesiologies have been tested and worked out within a particular historical set of circumstances. So the aim here has not been to theorize about Christian approaches to violence or Marxism, nor to propose theologies which might be appropriate in hypothetical revolutionary situations, but to discover how believers responded to a concrete process with which they were confronted. Whether their experience will prove prototypical remains to be seen but, as an example of what can happen to the church in a revolutionary situation it helped partly to create, it raises a number of practical and theoretical questions of interest to all concerned about the church's mission and witness in the real world it is called to serve.

Much of the research for this book was undertaken while I was doing some postgraduate study in the Department of Theology and Religious Studies at Bristol University. Financial support was provided by the British Academy, whose help in this respect I should like to acknowledge. I owe a debt of gratitude of a rather different sort to my supervisor at Bristol, Dr Denys Turner, who first aroused my interest in Nicaragua and whose wise counsel and constructive appraisal of my efforts I very much valued. Thanks are also due to the following individuals and organizations who responded most helpfully to my requests for material: the Catholic Institute for International Relations, the Nicaragua Solidarity Campaign, the Carila Resource Centre, Marigold Best of Quaker Peace and Service, Sister Goodyer of the Catholic Media Office, Simon Barrow of the Church Missionary Society, the British Council of Churches, the Central America Information Service, Church Action for Central America, the Evangelical Union of South America, Keston College, the Latin America Bureau, the editors of *Third Way* and *The Tablet*, and the Bristol University Catholic Chaplaincy.

I also wish to thank a number of friends who assisted in many different ways with this project: Nick Stevens, Pauline Johns, Sally Meek, Cynthia Melillo, Roger Vince, Juanita Jiménez, Jonathan Peters and, in a special way, Jackie Edwards. I also valued the advice and encouragement given by the Editor of Epworth Press, Rev. John Stacey. Finally, special thanks to my parents who also helped in many different and sometimes intangible ways, particularly since the work of preparing the final manuscript was undertaken during a summer spent at home. I should like to dedicate this book to them. Needless to say, none of those mentioned above shares any responsibility for this work, nor necessarily endorses anything it contains.

Eliot College   AWB
University of Kent at Canterbury
January 1987

Abbreviations

ACLEN	Asociación del Clero Nicaragüense (Nicaraguan Clergy Association)
AMPRONAC	Asociación de Mujeres ante la Problemática Nacional (Association of Women Confronting the National Problem)
ATC	Asociación de Trabajadores del Campo (Association of Rural Workers)
CAV	Centro Ecumenico Antonio Valdivieso (Antonio Valdivieso Ecumenical Centre)
CDS	Comités de Defensa Sandinista (Sandinista Defence Committees)
CEBs	comunidades eclesiales de base (basic Christian communities)
CELAM	Consejo Episcopal Latinoamericano (Latin American Episcopal Council)
CEPA	Centro de Educación y Promoción Agrícola (Centre for Rural Education and Development)
FAO	Frente Amplio de Oposición (Broad Opposition Front)
FSLN	Frente Sandinista de Liberación Nacional (Sandinista National Liberation Front)
UDEL	Unión Democrática de Liberación (Democratic Union for Liberation)

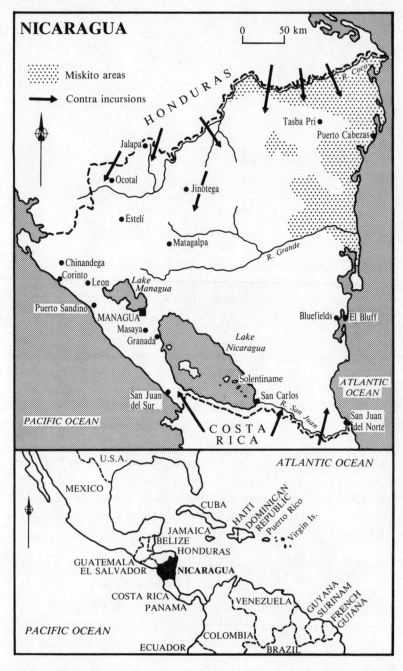

1 · The Church in Latin America: From an Alliance with Power to an Option for the Poor

In the 1950s the suggestion would have been considered rash and ill-informed that within two decades the church in parts of Latin America would be promoting revolutionary change and, in one country, actually participating in a successful insurrection. All the evidence of history pointed against it for, since the Catholic church first established itself in the region, it had shown little appetite for economic or social reform, but rather a commitment to defend the existing order and resist any change which threatened its own position and influence. As late as 1959 the overthrow of Batista in Cuba found the church, at first uncommitted, taking sides before long with the opposition to the revolutionary government. Its conservative roots ran so deeply into the soil of many centuries that only an earthquake of some force appeared sufficient to shift them. Yet the picture that emerged from Nicaragua in the late 1970s suggests that a convulsion of sorts did take place, and a consideration of the causes and scope of this phenomenon will provide a necessary introduction to the developments to be discussed in the following chapters.

Catholicism arrived in Latin America on a wave of Spanish colonial expansion at the beginning of the sixteenth century. Among the *conquistadores* in search of new sources of wealth came others with a more missionary spirit, for whom the securement of souls for the King of Kings was no less important than the acquisition of land and gold for the king of Spain. Among the Maya and Aztec Indians on the Central American isthmus they found a thriving and deeply-rooted religious culture which, because they were unable to overcome or eradicate it completely, they infused with their own brand of European Christianity. Evangelization was rapid but often quite superficial, and even today, though most of the population claims formal membership of the Catholic church, the influence of the old folk religion still remains.

The strong religiosity of the people has rendered the church a powerful agent in Latin American society, though historically it exercised its power more to reinforce and legitimize the values of the prevailing ideology than to defend the interests of the masses. For over three hundred years following the conquest its fatalistic and highly spiritualized form of Christianity played an effective part in maintaining the semi-feudal structures of the old colonial order. It became locked in a symbiotic relationship with the civil authorities who granted it status, wealth and influence, particularly through the educational system, in return for the church's unequivocal support. The price of this support included the hierarchy's losing its right to engage in prophetic denunciation of injustice and oppression, thus leaving it open to charges of complicity in such excesses. In cultivating close ties with the élites the church became increasingly remote in the eyes of the people, a problem compounded by a perpetual shortage of clergy. Yet the majority maintained at least nominally their allegiance to the faith it had once taught them.

To speak of 'the church' is not to suggest that it was a monolithic structure, for there were also those within it at all levels on whom the charge of indifference to poverty and suffering could not be made to stick. Some of the original missionaries and religious developed a rather different model of the church, one that situated itself among the people, and men and women like Bartolomé de Las Casas, Juan del Valle and the martyred bishop of Nicaragua, Antonio Valdivieso, became known as 'saviours of the Indians' through their efforts in the service of the people and the defence of their rights. Such people, though always a minority, formed what Míguez Bonino has called 'the fountainhead of a small but never interrupted stream of prophetic protest in Latin American Christianity',[1] a stream which, by the latter half of the twentieth century, had opened up into a swift torrent.

In the nineteenth century, with the influx of new liberal ideologies from Europe, the Catholic church went into a decline. In the drive for political independence and greater freedom of trade the old colonial order began to collapse, weakening all that had held it together, including the church. Exposed as a reactionary and increasingly anachronistic institution, its influence waned rapidly, and the new breed of liberal governments in the newly-independent states of Central America took steps to ensure it would not easily recover it. In Nicaragua the government of José Santos Zelaya (1893–1909) effected a separation of church and state, exiling many bishops and priests and suppressing the religious orders. These new liberal governments also encouraged Protestant churches to establish themselves in the region, not only to weaken Catholic influence but also because Puritan values were considered more compatible with the new emphasis on liberty, morality and individual enterprise. Like Catholicism before it, Protestantism thus came to support and be identified with the prevailing ideology, in this case liberal capitalism. It never had the mass impact of Catholicism, however, and though its size and influence is growing, it embraces today perhaps no more than five per cent of the population of Central America.

It was not until after the First World War that the Latin American church really began to come to terms with the new political and economic order. Initially attracted by fashionable corporatist ideologies, it sought to strengthen its traditional ties with conservative political groups, but its emphasis moved, especially after the Second War, to evangelization and social reform. Under the banner of Catholic Action, lay-people were motivated to begin reasserting the church's influence in the region through the formation of grass-roots organizations like labour unions and Christian Democratic parties. The establishment of Catholic universities also brought the church back into the field of education. This activity, which drew much of its inspiration from the work of French thinkers like Jacques Maritain, was both a reaction to growing Protestant and humanist influence in the region, and a drive towards the 're-Christianization' of society, this time from below. In effect the old 'Christendom' ideal of a dominant church imposing Christianity from above was being replaced by a newer model (sometimes referred to as neo-Christendom), which had the same vision of society but attempted its

3

realization through social and cultural projects and individual Christian effort on the ground.

In the Cold War era of the 1950s this programme of social action intensified further as the church joined the crusade to halt the relentless forward march of Communism. Strengthened by an influx of foreign priests and a new-found unity reflected in the formation of a General Bishops' Conference (CELAM) in 1955, the church began to establish a significant presence among the poor in the cities and rural areas. Leaving their parishes in the better areas of the capital cities, many priests and religious moved out into the countryside to confront, in many cases for the first time, the life-style endured by the vast majority of their flock: the hard labour for low pay, the high levels of infant mortality, the shortage of essential services, and the powerlessness of the people to bring about any change for the better. It was an important turning point in the history of the Latin American church.

The church's encounter with the peasants (or *campesinos*) stimulated a dialectical learning process known as *concientización*[2] in which, by working alongside the poor, the missionaries came to understand more deeply their situation and, in turn, endeavoured to bring them to an understanding of the causes of their conditions and the possibilities for change. Drawing heavily on the teaching of the Brazilian educationist Paulo Freire they sought to demythologize the social order and encourage an awareness in the people that their poverty was not divinely ordained but rooted in the prevailing political and economic arrangements which, being human creations, could be subject to change. To the authorities this was nothing short of political indoctrination, and they absorbed each wave of protest with half-hearted reform or outright repression. But the process of *concientización* continued to grow, so that the church emerged in many parts of Latin America as the major political opposition and an 'umbrella' for weaker organs of protest. As such it became increasingly a target of government hostility and was accused of Communist subversion. Considering what had originally motivated its concern for the poor, this was no small irony. The effect, however, was generally to strengthen its resolve, and on the anvil of adversity was being forged a more socially conscious church.

The 1960s proved to be a decade of profound change for the church in Latin America. Whilst some in the hierarchy remained committed to the old colonial-church model, a growing body of opinion was acknowledging the need for a radical reappraisal of the role and mission of the church in an undeveloped yet basically Christian region. The experience of 'going to the poor' had aroused in many clergy and pastoral workers not only a renewed missionary zeal but also a sense of guilt over what they saw as the church's past support for unjust and repressive systems. This support, they argued, must end, and a commitment to social and economic change in the interests of the poor should now characterize the church.

The Second Vatican Council, which met between 1962 and 1965, gave significant encouragement, direction and authentication to this still inchoate process of reassessment in Latin America. At the Council the church put aside its traditional claim to be the exclusive locus of divine grace in the world, and its previous self-image as a transcendent self-enclosed society impervious to the shifting values around it, and redefined itself as an essentially human community, a 'pilgrim people'. It identified itself with the joys, hopes, sorrows and anxieties of all, especially the poor and suffering, and spoke of its commitment to the task of establishing peace and international justice and its desire to co-operate in building a universal brotherhood. This new emphasis had a number of consequences for Latin American Catholics: the church became less concerned with roles and hierarchies and placed greater importance on lay activity; it became free, at least in theory, from its previous identification with conservative politics; and it recognized that working to achieve peace and justice in the world would involve the church in co-operation and dialogue with all groups, including those which explicitly rejected or opposed it.

No less relevant to the Latin American church was the concern also expressed by the Council to see greater economic parity, both within and between nations, as the basis for restoring human dignity, social justice and world peace. In its *Pastoral Constitution on the Church in the World of Today (Gaudium et Spes*, 1965), the Council identified an 'excessive concern for profit', 'excessive social and economic inequalities' and, in certain cases, 'economic and social structures' as obstacles to peace and harmony, and also emphasized the importance of production for social use, the social responsibility of private ownership, and the right of those in need 'to supply this need from the riches of others'. It did not go so far as to advocate

5

violence or insurrection to promote change, although in his encyclical *Populorum Progressio* published two years later Pope Paul VI did tentatively admit the possibility of 'revolutionary uprising . . . where there is manifest, long-standing tyranny which would do great damage to fundamental personal rights and dangerous harm to the common good of the country . . .'

The Council's conclusions, and its call to the church to examine the signs of the times, found a ready response in Latin America. Many Christians, adopting the prevailing economic theory that the 'development' of the continent could be achieved with aid from the developed world, deepened their commitment to work towards that goal. Christian Democratic parties were widely supported as agents of peaceful social reform, a sort of *tercerista* or third way between the failed capitalism of the past and the sudden and perhaps violent upheaval envisaged by Marxism. The programme of *concientización* also received fresh impetus, and in countries with a particularly acute shortage of clergy, like Nicaragua, groups of lay workers known as Delegates of the Word were especially trained and commissioned for this work among the rural poor. Delegates also played a significant role in strengthening and developing the small grass-roots communities which were springing up in the wake of the *concientización* process and the new links forged between the church and the people. As closely-knit groups of Christians living, working and sharing together, these base communities (*comunidades eclesiales de base* or CEBs) played a major part in the work of *concientización* and were to provide also a new model for the church in Latin America.

In time many Christians in these communities and elsewhere in the church began increasingly to reject the development model of economic growth, especially as it became apparent that the foreign aid programmes which had promised so much were having a negative rather than positive effect on general living standards. Kennedy's Alliance for Progress, for example, a large-scale invest-ment and aid programme designed to stimulate and modernize the Latin American economy, was seen to have benefited only margin-ally the mass of the people and effectively to have widened the gap between rich and poor. Instead there arose a growing conviction that the economies of the Latin American countries were geared almost entirely to serving the needs and wants of the major world powers, and that the position of these countries *vis–à-vis* the First World was more accurately to be understood in terms of economic *dependence*. The way forward was therefore seen to be not through more programmes of development, nor through the reformism of Christian Democracy, but in complete 'liberation' from economic captivity.

A re-reading of the Bible in the light of this commitment to liberation has given rise to a new way of doing theology in some parts of the church. This is usually referred to as 'liberation theology'. This does not set out to legitimize Christian involvement in the task of liberation but, taking that as its point of departure, provides a theological reflection on that involvement from within the process itself. It aims to be a practical or 'praxis-centred' rather than an academic theology (though the vast body of literature that it has generated has brought it perilously close to the latter), with interpretation of the biblical texts being undertaken only after, and in the light of, an active commitment to liberation. This reflection in turn informs and stimulates further praxis. Praxis is also informed by a critical and selective reading of Marx, whose scientific analysis of society is considered most helpful in suggesting how the goal of the kingdom of God may be built within history. In liberation theology traditional Christian concepts are present, but become infused with new meaning in the light of a commitment to liberation. Thus sin, for example, is not confined to the area of private moral behaviour but can also be manifested in the structures of an unjust society, and correspondingly God's redemptive activity extends beyond the individual to the liberation of historical communities. To love one's neighbour, as Gutiérrez puts it, is to work for a 'classless society without owners and dispossessed, without oppressors and oppressed', in which love can be made truly authentic.[3] Such reinterpretation plays a major part in the *concientización* process by releasing Christian symbols and concepts from their (no less ideological) use in the past to ensure the subservience of the mass of believers to church and state.

By the time the Second General Conference of Latin American bishops convened at Medellín, Colombia, in 1968 to apply the principles of Vatican II to their region, it was clear that there was some degree of support for a vision of political and economic liberation at every level of the church. Whereas the interpretative framework of Vatican II had been decidedly developmentalist, the

Medellín documents, in affirming the bishops' commitment to the full liberation of the poor, reflected their conversion to the dependence model. This was also evidenced by the different methodology adopted at Medellín, for whereas Vatican II spoke in general terms of progress and transformation in an apparently neutral ideological framework, the Latin American bishops began with an analysis of the situation they encountered, where injustice was incarnate in the structures of society, and moved from there to consider theological principles and possible responses. In many ways these responses endorsed the pastoral work already in progress on the ground: for example, encouragement was given to the development of the CEBs, to a *concientización* 'ordered to changing the structures', and to the use of education for 'liberating the masses from all servitude' and 'equipping them (to be) authors of their own progress'.

Though it became a central topic of debate in Latin America, liberation theology, like the base communities which helped to shape it, was no more than a minority interest in the 1960s. In terms of popularity and activism its followers were well matched by groups on the 'right' of the church, notably the Societies for the Defence of Tradition, Family and Property, which were committed to reversing all post-conciliar change. It is doubtful, too, whether the tenor of the Medellín conclusions reflected a majority view in the Latin American church at that time, and even the 146 bishops who attended the conference may not have been representative of the hierarchy as a whole. Indeed, in some parts of the church there was a considerable backlash against the Medellín recommendations, and some of the bishops who had originally supported them also began to back-pedal when they realized that they were being used to endorse some extreme programmes not envisaged at the time. There was evidence of a tension between 'conservatives' and 'progressives' within CELAM at its ordinary conference in Sucre, Bolivia in 1972 and during the build-up to the Third General Conference at Puebla, Mexico in 1979, though the final document from this latter conference did reaffirm the 'preferential option for the poor' that the bishops had made at Medellín. Some observers have suggested that one explanation for the radical analysis adopted by the bishops at Medellín, and their subsequent failure to translate it into a positive programme, may be the religious and political background against which the conference was held – the publication of *Populorum Progressio* the year before, and the general mood of radicalism abroad which found expression in the Paris student unrest and the anti-Vietnam demonstrations. Yet even allowing for its historical context, for a conference of Latin American bishops to express unequivocally a 'solidarity with the poor', after centuries of hierarchical support for systems which militated against them, represented not just a mere political realignment but an attempt fundamentally to reappraise the nature of the church in a post-colonial yet still economically dependent situation.

As the decade of change drew to a close, many questions raised by this concern with reappraisal remained before the church, to which Vatican II and Medellín had offered only partial answers. To what extent was the church prepared not only to opt *for* the poor but also to lose its long-held privileges and become a church *of* the poor – how far, in other words, would the CEBs become a future model for the church? Would the church's commitment to the poor be translated into concrete projects or remain at the level of general guidelines and principles? Should the church always avoid identifying with secular or humanist programmes of liberation in order to preserve its independent prophetic voice? Should ecumenism now be based on a commitment to the struggle for liberation rather than on issues of doctrine or church order? Would the church's opposition to unjust social and economic structures lead it also to work towards transforming those structures? Up to what point could the church continue to oppose the use of violent means to combat the structural or 'institutionalized' violence which Medellín identified as the cause of so much suffering in Latin America? Could the church continue to maintain at all costs a unity, and a claim to speak for all, in the face of opposing ideological strands within it (for example the CEBs on one side and those who 'opted out' of Medellín's option for the poor on the other), or would it recognize that, in the struggle for liberation, class conflict must of necessity occur within its ranks as well as in society at large? Should it, in Hugo Assmann's words, 'no longer accept that eucharistic conditions can automatically obtain in a Church that includes oppressors and oppressed'?[4]

It was with questions such as these that the churches in Central America became increasingly concerned in the 1970s, not in some abstract or theoretical way but as they confronted the reality around

9

them. In Nicaragua they were to coalesce into one single dilemma: how should the church respond when a revolutionary programme, embodying the social and economic transformation for which it has called but over whose execution it has not ultimate control, appears historically realizable?

2 · The Church Militant

Nicaragua is the largest state in Central America, but although it is approximately the size of England and Wales its population barely exceeds three million. Of these, four per cent are 'pure-blooded' Indians living mostly on the Atlantic coast, while the remainder are largely *mestizos* whose mixed Spanish and Indian blood bears permanent testimony to the three centuries of colonial rule which ended with formal independence in 1821. The Catholic church continues to embrace the vast majority of Nicaraguans, although the number of Protestants, who are more commonly referred to as 'evangelicals', has grown to represent perhaps fifteen per cent of the population.

The modern history of the country can be distilled into two words, *somocismo* and *sandinismo*, Spanish terms for the ideologies which have profoundly affected the lives of all Nicaraguan people for the last fifty years. The former derives from the name of the family which exercised an unbroken dictatorship over the country for forty-three years, the latter from the guerrilla leader, Augusto César Sandino, whose undefeated campaign against the US marines in the 1920s and 1930s inspired the movement which was instrumental in overthrowing the Somoza dynasty in 1979, the Frente Sandinista de Liberación Nacional (FSLN). Ironically Sandino's resistance led indirectly to the rise of the Somozas, for as the US troops withdrew from Nicaragua in 1933 they left in charge the head of the National Guard, Anastasio Somoza García, who, within three years, disposed of Sandino and his followers, consolidated his control over the Liberal Party and assumed the presidency.

Despite short periods when the presidency formally moved

outside the family, the Somozas effectively maintained control of Nicaragua until 1979, through first Somoza García, who was assassinated in 1956, and then his sons Luis (who died from a heart attack in 1967) and Anastasio II. Whereas the styles and qualities of the two brothers differed – Luis was perhaps more democratic, liberal and committed to social reform than 'Tachito', who tended to rely rather more on military power – both ran the country as if it were their own personal estate. Through their control of a vast range of companies, banks, farms and other concerns the family amassed a huge fortune, much of it invested outside Nicaragua.

For most Nicaraguans life under *somocismo* was poor, nasty, brutish and short, for the economic inequality it generated was, by any objective criteria, extreme. Whereas half the country's farmland was owned by fewer than two hundred families, the poorer half of the farming population shared less than four per cent, and 200,000 people had no land at all. Somoza's own holding was 5,000,000 acres, an area almost the size of El Salvador. In 1972 the average income of the poorer half of the rural population was around $35 per annum, which left them some way behind the Somozas, whose personal fortune was estimated at the time of the revolution to be in excess of $500 million. In 1976 a United Nations survey discovered that fifty per cent of all registered deaths in Nicaragua were of children under five, and of the children of that age still living fifty-seven per cent were malnourished. In short, while a small number of families lived in luxury, the majority, especially in the countryside, faced acute shortages of essential services like health care, good housing, running water and, the key which might have released them from their dehumanizing impoverishment, education.

For many years the church appears to have maintained a silence about this state of affairs and lent its support to the dictatorship. The view expressed by four bishops in a pastoral letter in 1930 advising Sandino and his troops to 'abandon sterile armed struggles, return to the life of home and work and to the fulfilment of religious duties' may well be representative of the hierarchy's attitude throughout most of the Somoza years. Only three years before, Bishop Canuto Reyes y Balladares had blessed the weapons of the US marines as they set out to do battle with Sandino's forces. In 1942, in a ceremony in the national stadium, Archbishop Lezcano crowned Somoza's daughter queen of the army with a crown borrowed from the statue of the Virgin at Candelaria. In a pastoral letter in 1950 the bishops reminded their flock that all authority has a divine origin and that therefore to obey the ruler is ultimately to obey God. In 1956 Somoza García was buried as a 'prince of the church' with only one bishop, Calderón y Padilla of Matagalpa, declining to attend the ceremony in protest. Archbishop González offered two hundred days' indulgence to those Catholics assisting with prayers for the departed ruler. A US Catholic Press Association report in 1962 observed that the church had virtually abandoned the countryside where over half the population lived, and was living in the past, blind to social problems, and identified with a government 'hated by the people'. Whilst it could be argued that the bishops were not consciously legitimating a disreputable dictatorship, since traditionally the church teaches respect for authorities which permit religious freedom, it is noteworthy that even until 1978, when Somoza was attacking all opposition to him including churches and religious communities, the bishops continued to attend the inauguration of parliament to invite divine guidance on its proceedings.

The fact that by 1979 all sections of the church were found supporting the final insurrection demonstrates that within a relatively short period it had undergone quite a transformation. Some of the roots of that process will now be explored, but it is important to stress at this stage that any attempt to understand properly its response to the revolution must first recognize the heterogeneous nature of the Nicaraguan church. Though it is often convenient shorthand, it is in fact misleading to speak of 'the church' supporting or turning against the revolution, since it seldom responded to events in a united way. Thus it will not be possible to identify in the church's response to the revolution a single unified process; it is, rather, a patchwork of different responses born of a variety of experiences, perceptions and theological approaches. So what processes led to sections of the church becoming committed to the revolution, and what explanations might there be for the differing degrees of response within the church as a whole?

For some Christians a commitment to revolutionary struggle followed a period of *concientización* and biblical reflection in the base communities. Often the ones who had experienced first-hand the poverty generated under *somocismo*, these Christians were encouraged within the CEBs to lose their fatalistic assumptions about the

13

causes of their condition and believe that they could work for their own liberation. Ernesto Cardenal has confirmed that this was the purpose behind his famous community established in 1966 at Solentiname on Lake Nicaragua, and the transcripts of its dialogues which he has edited and published[1] demonstrate how important theological reflection proved to be in developing a political consciousness. In their discussions on the weekly gospel the Solentiname *campesinos* unselfconsciously and almost empathetically identified their own conditions with those of first-century Palestine, drawing parallels, for example, between the 'atmosphere of terror and repression' which they believed provided the context for Jesus' ministry and their own situation under Somoza (Herod) and the 'gringo ambassador' (Pilate). The most powerful images were taken from the life and ministry of Christ himself, who was seen as the liberator and instigator of revolution, bringing a 'political manifesto' of release to the captives and liberty to the oppressed (Luke 4.18–30), and a subversive kingdom of unity, justice, equality and love. Cardenal encouraged his community to see parallels between this kingdom and Communist society, sometimes using Cuba (which he had visited) as a concrete example, to counteract official government teaching that Communism was inherently evil: 'The Communists try to achieve a perfect society where each one contributes his labour and receives according to his needs', he said during one discussion: '. . . in the Gospels they were already teaching that.' The ultimate cost of working to establish a better society may be death – as in the case of Jesus and Sandino – but not defeat, for the resurrection symbolizes the final victory of life over death. A common slogan in revolutionary Nicaragua was 'Sandino *vive*' (Sandino lives), a reference to the resumption and eventual victory of the struggle for which he died.

The effect of this tendency towards what many would regard as theological reductionism was, as Cardenal himself recognized, a more social and political Christianity among members of the Solentiname community: 'When these young people are so concerned for the liberation of their people,' he later said, 'and for things like better health, better education, better housing, then they are less concerned about the things of heaven. I think Christ will understand that.'[2]

In response to *concientización* of this type a number of base community members became involved in political protest and revolutionary activity, believing that only through organized collective action could they achieve a new society. Christians from the San Pablo community in Managua, founded by Fr José de la Jara about the same time as Solentiname, were instrumental in an early protest against bus fare increases, and Fr Uriel Molina's community in the Rigueiro *barrio* (district) staged a similar action against a milk price rise in the capital. Several members of this community had also participated in an occupation of the cathedral in Managua in 1970 to protest against the arrest and detention without trial of some fellow students from the Catholic university. In December 1973, at a mass attended by Somoza to mark the first anniversary of the earthquake in Managua, hundreds of base community members from the city smuggled anti-régime placards into the service, helping to provoke the dictator into leaving prematurely in disgust. In 1976 a CEB founded by the Maryknoll Sisters in the OPEN 3 *barrio* in Managua organized a successful three-month campaign against increases in water rates which had been imposed on the poorer, but not the more affluent, areas of the city. Solentiname eventually became involved in armed struggle when, in 1977, some of its members participated in an FSLN attack on a National Guard outpost in the nearby town of San Carlos. Two lost their lives, and shortly afterwards the Guard attacked the community, destroying most of its buildings.

It is difficult to assess fully how significant the *concientización* work undertaken in these communities was to the overall revolutionary process. Clearly, many Christians owed their new-found awareness and revolutionary commitment to the community dialogues and Bible studies, and some, like Luis Carrión from *barrio* Rigueiro, and Cardenal himself, went on to become leading members of the FSLN. The initiative in this process often came from the Front itself, which recognized the leadership experience many Delegates and other Christians had gained in the CEBs, and actually looked on these communities as (in Carrión's phrase) 'quarries' in their search for cadres. The CEBs also had very strong links with the popular grass-roots organizations which were springing up and which were to play a major role in preparing people for revolutionary involvement. These organizations were more overtly political in their intent and, although they had no direct links with the church, attracted large numbers of Christians whose involvement often received official church approval. In some places the overlap in membership was such that the popular organizations were barely distinguishable

15

from the CEBs. Christians were also involved in leading some of these organizations, and the Association of Rural Workers (ATC), formed by the FSLN in 1977, numbered among its original directors some key people from the Centre for Rural Education and Development (CEPA), a body very closely involved with the CEBs. Through their involvement in these organizations the CEBs exerted a significant influence on the revolutionary process. Overall, though the communities embraced only a minority of the country's Christians, by their *concientización* work, leadership training, and participation in the popular organizations, they had an impact disproportionate to their size. After the revolution the FSLN officially recognized the sacrifice made by many Delegates of the Word in the struggle, and on another occasion acknowledged that but for the process of consciousness-raising they undertook, the revolution could not have succeeded.

A less structured process of consciousness-raising also took place outside the CEBs as many Christians became increasingly alienated by the activities of Somoza and the Guard, and more convinced that responsibility for conditions in the country lay directly with the dictatorship. In the 1960s the *Cursillos de Christiandad* (Short Courses on Christianity) movement, whose teaching was focused upon themes in liberation theology, had radicalized some middle-class church people, but it was their experience of extreme aspects of *somocismo* which proved for many the real turning point. Somoza's reaction to the 1972 Managua earthquake, which killed over ten thousand people and displaced tens of thousands more, was symbolic: while many Christians engaged in relief work in the city, he and the Guard diverted large amounts of foreign aid sent in response to the disaster into their own accounts, and Somoza then secured further financial advantage through land speculation and by awarding himself contracts for reconstruction work. For many Christians the structural sin referred to by the Latin American bishops at Medellín had begun to take concrete shape in the form of *somocismo*.

The earthquake was also an important turning point for many evangelicals, who had not experienced a Vatican II- or Medellín-type awakening. Involvement in relief work and development programmes established a greater unity between the various denominations, and between evangelicals and Catholics, and began a process of growing political awareness which led many, including some pastors, eventually to support the revolution and join or collaborate with the FSLN.

As opposition to Somoza gradually intensified during the 1970s, so churches and Christian communities assumed an increasingly important role as places of refuge for those under threat from the régime. In this way they became in many areas foci of popular resistance to Somoza and themselves targets for attack, though the effect in general was to deepen their hostility to the régime. The Capuchin Fathers, who had trained the original Delegates of the Word, and individual priests like Fernando Cardenal and Miguel D'Escoto, also played a significant role in documenting and publicizing abroad the human rights situation under Somoza. The growing public opposition of the church to the régime also brought it into closer contact with the FSLN, a contact which deepened still further as the Front, lacking in many areas a grass-roots party structure of its own, increasingly adopted the parish structure of the church as an organizational base for its own activities.

Although opposition to Somoza among Christians was to grow to the point where Catholics from all sections of the church eventually participated in the final insurrection, until the final stages of the campaign only a minority actually became members of the FSLN. One reason was that the Front was not the only channel through which political opposition could be expressed, and it did not achieve hegemony in the revolutionary struggle until less than a year before the revolution. For some Christians, too, the Marxist element in its leadership made it unattractive in a climate where traditional attitudes towards Communism were very black-and-white. There were also Christians who, whilst strongly opposed to Somoza, held right to the end a hope that some compromise solution could be worked out without resort to violent struggle and, by implication, the involvement of the FSLN.

Yet among those who did take the overtly political step of joining or collaborating with the Sandinistas in the early and mid-1970s, many considered their action to be entirely consistent with their profession of the Christian faith. Fernando Cardenal, a Jesuit priest who was later to play a prominent role in the revolutionary government, has affirmed that since he began working for the Front in 1973 he has met nothing which has contradicted or clashed with his Christian or moral beliefs – in fact quite the opposite. 'For me the Sandinista Front has been the channel that has enabled me to live my Christian faith more authentically, that is, with actions,' he states.[3] Cardenal claims that the impulse which led him to join the FSLN came from a meditation in depth on Jesus' parable of the Samaritan, in which he saw the Nicarguan people at the side of the road, 'wounded by exploitation and misery', and the FSLN as the good Samaritan who cared for the wounded victim. 'It seemed obvious to me,' he later recalled, 'that I ought not to be like that priest or that levite who continued along and abandoned the wounded man.'[4] Another priest and prominent Sandinista minister, Miguel D'Escoto, also attributed his decision to join the revolution to an interpretation of this parable. Both Cardenal and D'Escoto eventually made public their revolutionary commitment by joining a group of intellectuals and business-people known as *Los Doce* (the Twelve) which from 1977 played an important role in mobilizing opposition to Somoza. The Twelve advocated full participation by the FSLN in any solution to the crisis, and the resignation of Somoza as a precondition for dialogue.

Shortly after the destruction of Solentiname, Ernesto Cardenal declared that 'fidelity to the gospel' had led him, too, to join the FSLN. Echoing some words of Camilo Torres, the Colombian priest-guerrilla who was killed in combat in 1966, Cardenal described as a 'priestly struggle' the task of building a new society based on gospel principles. For Cardenal, like Torres, revolutionary struggle is priestly because it is about creating a situation in which charity can be carried out on a national rather than individual level and so become truly effective. Only with the revolution, Cardenal said during a Solentiname Bible study on the Last Judgment,

> could there be effective carrying out of works of mercy in society as a whole: to feed the hungry, give drink to the thirsty, clothe the naked, teach the ignorant, etc. In the past the saints, when a just society wasn't possible because of the means of production that were then in force (slavery, feudalism, or capitalism), what they did was to practise charity individually or through a small group: a religious society that they founded. But now Camilo Torres' effective charity is possible.[5]

Cardenal maintained that a commitment to build a just society, 'a real and concrete kingdom of God here on earth', was behind Solentiname's decision to join the San Carlos offensive, and the Spanish priest Gaspar García Laviana declared that a similar concern had led him also to take up arms and join the Sandinista Front.

Those priests who joined the FSLN claimed that the experience led them to a new and deeper understanding of their faith and traditional Christian doctrines. García, for example, argued that working to free the people from *somocismo* was like working to free them from sin. Luis Carrión said he 'drew near the revolution through a religious experience ... My first encounter with the concept of justice, my first search for identification with the people, took that road'.[6] For D'Escoto, taking part in the revolution was 'a most profound religious experience' because a new depth of unity was felt between the participants through their common commitment to die for the cause. 'I have never celebrated the Eucharist more meaningfully than when I celebrated it with my fellow freedom fighters,' he later recalled. Knowing that they themselves might have to suffer gave the words 'this is my body . . . this is my blood' a new dimension.

> We were making Christ's words our own. We were entering into his passion really. We were entering into his cross. Besides meaning *his* body, the words 'my body' meant my own body, too, which was also prepared to be sacrificed, and 'my blood' also meant my own blood, which was ready to be poured out, shed. There, right down inside me, I discovered an authentic disposition to live what the Eucharist signifies . . . For me the whole war was a great Eucharist . . .[7]

Fernando Cardenal's involvement with the FSLN brought him to a fresh – though, he claims, biblically orthodox – evaluation of 'faith' and 'atheism' in which correct praxis rather than explicit testimony to Christ is the criterion. 'In the Bible, the atheist is the one who doesn't love. That's who really denies God,' he has said. To Cardenal it is those who dedicate their lives to the cause of the poor, even without acknowledging God, who show genuine faith, and those who turn against the poor, even though they profess Christ, who deny God and meet the biblical definition of atheism. When forced to choose between these two positions, Cardenal confesses, 'I

19

prefer to be with those who, without putting God's name on their lips, and perhaps without even formally knowing God, are doing all God asks to be done for a suffering people.'[8] Other Sandinista priests, including Miguel D'Escoto and Edgar Parrales, have also embraced this position.

This belief that, as Gutiérrez puts it, 'To know God is to do justice,' is a common theme in liberation theology for which biblical support is claimed by reference, in particular, to the Old Testament prophetic writers. Jeremiah 22.15–16 is one example:

> Did not your father eat and drink and do justice and righteousness? Then it was well with him. He judged the cause of the poor and the needy; then it was well. Is not this to know me? says the LORD.

In this schema God does not exist outside his activity in the world and is therefore to be known, not in an abstract sense, but through active obedience to his will. As Míguez Bonino has summarized it, obedience is neither a consequence of knowledge of God nor a precondition for it – it *is* our knowledge of God. 'We know God in the synthetic act of responding to his demands.'[9] The question which remains, however, is how far this kind of hermeneutical approach leaves theology able to say or do anything not already being said or done by other ideologies or emancipatory movements. Can faith become anything more than a synonym for political or social activity to promote justice and the 'cause of the poor'?

Joining the Sandinista Front raised for D'Escoto and the Cardenal brothers the question how, as priests, they could accommodate themselves within a Marxist-led movement. They resolved the issue on two levels. In the first place they argued that Marxism is not *per se* incompatible with Christianity but can, as a scientific method for analysing and changing society, be of use in translating Christian ideals into reality. The gospel sets out the goal of social change, a new community based on love, but not the methods to use to attain it. 'So we have to have recourse to all the sciences that can help us,' says Fernando Cardenal, 'philosophy, physics, chemistry, engineering, the social sciences – and among the social sciences, Marxism.'[10] According to this thesis Marxism does not replace Christianity since the two appear to operate on different levels, and Christianity, by dictating the ends of political action to which

Marxism may be a means, remains the motivating factor. How far it is valid or possible to adopt this kind of separation may be a point of debate, since both Marxism and Christianity appear to recognize an internal relationship between goals and means. Yet the priests' position is not uncommon in Latin America where, as Míguez says, co-operation between Marxists and Christians does not come about after intellectual dialogue – 'the objective conditions prompt a common action, and it is within this co-operation that dialogue takes place.'[11]

Secondly the priests have argued that a Christian presence in the FSLN helped to bring about a shift in its ideological base away from straightforward Marxism-Leninism. Although the Front was Marxist and anti-clerical when founded in the early 1960s, the latter perhaps as a reaction to the church's identification with Somoza, the radicalism of many Christians in the 1970s eventually led it to alter its stance and recognize the church as an important factor in the struggle for liberation. In so doing, as D'Escoto later said, 'they realized they were wrong in believing that only a Marxist could be a revolutionary. Thus the Front acquired maturity and it became authentically Sandinista.'[12] Two Marxist co-founders of the FSLN, Carlos Fonseca Amador (who was killed in 1976) and Tomás Borge Martinez, have agreed that *sandinismo* is not rigidly Marxist-Leninist but incorporates, along with the thought of Sandino, strands of Marxism, Liberalism and Christianity. This position has also been endorsed by other leading Sandinistas including Victor Tirado and Daniel Ortega.

For Christians who joined the FSLN the decision involved acknowledging that some recourse to violence would be inevitable if *somocismo* were to be removed, and for some this position appears to have been reached only after a recognition that pacifism could not ultimately succeed. Fernando Cardenal was involved in non-violent action like the occupation of the cathedral in 1970, but by 1973 had decided it was too late even for sustained pressure of the type advocated by Gandhi and Martin Luther King to be effective. 'I came to see more deeply and realistically, with each passing day, that the country no longer had any option but armed struggle,' he later recalled.[13] Ernesto Cardenal and Gaspar García experienced a similar transition. 'We recalled that Gandhi had said that in certain circumstances his doctrine of nonviolence couldn't be put into practice,' Ernesto later said. 'In Hitler's Germany it could not have been put into practice, and it was the same in Somoza's Nicaragua.'[14] García, who actually became a *comandante* in the FSLN and was killed in combat in 1978, claimed support for his position from the Medellín documents and the papal encyclical *Populorum Progressio* which appeared to endorse a revolutionary uprising where there is 'manifest, long-standing tyranny'. In fact at Medellín the bishops expressed grave reservations about the use of violence to effect political change, as they did at Puebla just a few months before the Nicaraguan revolution. However, the emphasis at both conferences on 'institutionalized violence' did suggest the possibility of a distinction, made explicit by a Peruvian bishops' congress in 1969, between 'the *unjust violence* of the oppressors (who maintain this despicable system)' and 'the *just violence* of the oppressed (who feel obliged to use it to achieve their liberation)'.[15]

For those Christians who considered that in Somoza's Nicaragua they were, as Medellín had put it, 'faced with a situation of injustice that can be called institutionalized violence' it became impossible to avoid involvement with violence whatever response they made. It would have to be part of any action to change the social structures, while to hold back from such action was effectively to side with those enforcing them, and therefore neutrality was impossible. For Fernando Cardenal the necessity of partisanship was obvious in a country,

> governed for nearly half a century by an unjust, murderous, bloody dictatorship, one that eradicated whole families . . . Either you're with the slaughtered or you're with the slaughterers. From a gospel point of view I don't think there was any other legitimate option we could have made.[16]

In such a situation it appears that it is not only violence but non-violence which has to be justified.

By 1978 most Christians were opposed to the Somoza régime, and many were also aligning themselves with the Sandinistas. At least three factors contributed to this. One was the continued harassment of Christian communities by the National Guard which did little to weaken their resistance to the régime and led many into closer collaboration with the Sandinistas. A second was the policy of the Catholic hierarchy to discourage this sort of collaboration, which also had little effect and led to one influential Jesuit movement, the Centre for Rural Education and Development (CEPA), becoming independent of the church and closely linked with the Sandinistas. But perhaps the most significant factor was the assassination in January 1978 of Pedro Joaquín Chamorro. As editor of *La Prensa* and a leader of the Democratic Union for Liberation (UDEL), the umbrella anti-Somoza organization, Chamorro was perhaps the most prominent opposition figure in Nicaragua at the time. His paper had become increasingly outspoken on human rights issues, and had been running a story about the activities of the blood export company Plasmaferesis in which the Somozas were believed to be stockholders. Chamorro had also had some contact with the FSLN. Whilst responsibility for his death may not have rested directly with Somoza, the event provoked a massive demonstration of anti-government feeling, and became for many the point at which they replaced mere opposition to the régime with a commitment to promote revolutionary change. Women in particular, including many from the CEBs, became more radicalized, and the Association of Women Confronting the National Problem (AM-PRONAC), which was already campaigning on human rights issues, was among those staging occupations and demonstrations. Overall, Somoza's increasing hostility to any political change continued to polarize the country and rapidly close up any middle way of reform that might have once been open in the past.

There is an apparent ambiguity in the relationship between the people and the FSLN, and between the FSLN and the revolution, which raises doubts about how significant formal membership of the Front was as an indication of support for its programme. Whilst it clearly united the mass of Nicaraguan people in the final overthrow of Somoza, it was never a vanguard party but rather a loose alliance of popular organizations and guerrilla groups. Commenting on events in the Monimbó *barrio* in Masaya in February 1978, when Christians participated in an armed response to a tear-gas attack by the National Guard, *barrio* member María Chavarría declared that it was only when FSLN militants arrived after the start of the action that 'we realized that *we* were the Frente Sandinista; that they would give guidance but that it was us, alongside them, who had to fight'.[17] Perhaps in this sense can one understand the comment made by one priest towards the end of the

23

insurrection that 'everyone was Christian and everyone was a Sandinista'.

Within the church perhaps the most complex response to the revolutionary process came from the Catholic hierarchy. Until the early 1970s, with the notable exception of Calderón y Padilla, the bishops had shown little inclination to end their long-standing connections with the Somoza régime and respond to Medellín's option for the poor. In 1969, the year after Medellín, a conference of Nicaraguan priests and religious identified 'a conservative and divided hierarchy, distant from the people and without initiative' presiding over a very remote and apathetic church. Yet the relationship between hierarchy and régime was beginning to cool; a clear indication of this was the appointment in late 1970 of Miguel Obando y Bravo as Archbishop of Managua in preference to a candidate proposed by the president. Obando declined to accept Somoza's offer of a Mercedes Benz car,[18] and then offended the dictator further by refusing to endorse the coalition government appointed in 1972. This had resulted from a pact between Somoza and the Conservative leader Fernando Agüero, but was widely seen as a device by which the former, constitutionally forbidden to stand for re-election as president, could retain real power until the next elections in 1974.

Further signs of a new stance by the hierarchy were evident in their pastoral letters. Obando's first letter as archbishop spoke of the church's commitment to denounce injustice and work towards a peaceful transformation of society, and in June 1971 the bishops voiced popular concerns about the distribution of wealth and 'organizational structures' in the country. In 1972 they criticized the new constitutional arrangements and echoed calls for a 'whole new order'. In February 1973, in the wake of the earthquake in Managua, the bishops suggested that the need for material reconstruction after the disaster symbolized the need for the construction also of a new and more just society. A few months later they issued a denunciation of the violence and abuse of human rights perpetrated by the government. At the end of 1973 Archbishop Obando used the mass organized to remember the Managua earthquake as an opportunity to criticize the dictatorship, offending the president to the extent that he walked out during the Archbishop's speech and had the National Guard unplug the amplification equipment. By January 1977 the bishops were warning of a 'state of terror' and denouncing the 'authorities' for their policy of imprisoning without trial, torture and summary execution. When the final offensive began the bishops spoke of a 'just insurrection', and Obando subsequently officiated at a victory mass, which might suggest that the hierarchy had continued to drift away from Somoza and adopt a stance in favour of revolutionary change. In fact their attitude to the régime, and to the revolution, proved at times rather ambivalent.

Three observations can be made from a study of the bishops' pronouncements and actions during this period. First they sometimes attempted to speak in non-specific terms and offer general principles which, though clearly intended to influence them, had no explicit connection with contemporary events. For example, their letter at the time of the Somoza-Agüero pact in 1972 talked in general terms of 'systematically shutting out other groups from access to public activity' and the effects of 'depriving the country of a necessary contrast in opposing viewpoints'. In two statements in 1974 they made a veiled reference to the National Guard by declaring that the 'military institution' should not serve particular interests, and spoke rather hypothetically about 'disorder' which results from a loss of freedom. One consequence of this practice was that interpretations of their position did not always agree. The 1972 letter, for example, was seen by some to contain a clear anti-dictatorial message, yet it also appeared to be warning Somoza that unless greater flexibility were introduced into the political system, groups such as the FSLN would flourish. If to sound such an alarm was their intention then the bishops could possibly be construed as acting in the dictator's *interests*. A pastoral letter of June 1978 was also initially seen as a belated attempt by the bishops to support armed revolution against Somoza, though in retrospect some doubted whether that had in fact been their intention. Not all the bishops' letters were couched in hypothetical terms, and their statements during Somoza's final years contained many pointed denunciations of his régime, but a tendency to adopt this style did characterize a number of their public messages both before and after the insurrection.

Secondly, the bishops attempted to cast the church in the role of mediator in the crisis. In many of their messages they denounced violence 'whatever its source' and frequently called for dialogue between the opposing factions. On two occasions when the FSLN staged successful commando raids detaining leading *somocistas* as hostages, in 1974 and 1978, Archbishop Obando acted as a go-between. Again, however, this was a policy open to varying interpretations. Whilst Obando's preparedness to negotiate with the FSLN appeared to gain the church some credibility in its eyes, some observers also argued that his mediation had no real significance since Somoza was forced to negotiate with the Front by virtue of the situation. The bishops' general condemnation of violence, and their calls for dialogue and co-existence, also attracted criticism on the grounds that they did not distinguish between aggressive and defensive violence, and failed to recognize that co-existence with Somoza would always be unequal – like 'the wolf with the lambs', as one critic put it.[19] The bishops did clarify their position on violence immediately before the insurrection, and in a statement of 2 June 1979 regretted 'the acts of violence that accompany the people's uprising' but drew a distinction between such acts whose 'moral and judicial lawfulness can no longer be denied' and the 'evident and endless tyranny' they aimed to overthrow. Archbishop Obando also declared a few days later that the war the people were waging was 'aimed against violence, and counterviolence is justified in a situation of permanent injustice'. As the conflict intensified in the weeks before Somoza was removed, the bishops perhaps recognized that a policy of conciliation had become increasingly incongruous, and the space for a mediatorial role rapidly reduced.

A third observation to note is the close correspondence between the hierarchy's position before the revolution and that of the anti-Somoza middle-class or bourgeoisie. In 1974, for example, when the opposition parties expressed their concern about the elections planned for that year, declaring, 'There's no one to vote for,' a pastoral letter from the bishops contained almost identical sentiments. Even more pronounced was the way in which both the hierarchy and the middle-class opposition promoted to the last a solution to the crisis which, although it would involve the removal of Somoza, would leave essentially intact the system he controlled – a sort of '*somocismo* without Somoza'. Even as the dictatorship was finally being overthrown, Obando was in Venezuela with leaders of the Broad Opposition Front (FAO) discussing plans for a non-revolutionary transfer of power to a broadly-based junta. In adopting

26

this position the hierarchy, like the middle-class opposition, refused to endorse the FSLN's position before the revolution and at times made veiled criticisms of their programme. This stance also distanced the hierarchy from those sections of the church moving gradually towards the Sandinistas, so that whilst a clear division had opened up during the 1970s between the church and the state, the rift *within* the church, between the revolutionary wing and the more moderate tendency led by the bishops, was perhaps the more profound of the two.

What explanations are there for these differences in attitude between the hierarchy and other sectors of the church? Two might usefully be considered: one socio-economic, the other ecclesiological. The first considers that the correspondence between the bishops' stance and that of the bourgeois opposition is not coincidental but reflects their similar class background. It suggests that although the position of the bishops may appear to emanate from a theological understanding of events, it rests fundamentally, like that of the secular opposition, on their economic and social position in society. This explanation would lead to the thesis that, although for a long time the bishops appeared neutral in wanting an end to all violence, they were in fact consciously giving support to conservative calls for a basic retention of the existing system.

Such an analysis not only offers a possible explanation for the bishops' position, but suggests that more radical Christian responses were not shaped primarily by religious impulses, though these were not insignificant, but by social and economic factors. In fact to revolutionary Christians subscribing to a theology of liberation such an analysis would not be unfamiliar, since it is a central tenet of this type of theology that no theologizing can be done in a vacuum or from detached contemplation but must emerge from concrete historical situations. Since there were clearly profound differences in their experience and perception of *somocismo* between the hierarchy and those 'concientized' in the base communities, a class explanation for their divergent responses to the revolution cannot be overlooked.

However, these divergent responses might also be attributable to different conceptions about the social role of the church. For example, those working among the CEBs would have held to a model of the church situated among the poor and open to the possibility of identification with specific political programmes and movements if the interests of the poor were perceived thereby to be better served. A recognition of the necessity of class conflict, both within and without the church, would be central to such a model, and would inevitably challenge the traditional hierarchical and authoritarian structures of the church. Influential among the hierarchy, however, appeared to be a more traditional understanding of the church. For the bishops the church has a duty to denounce evil in society and enunciate general principles and guidelines for action, but its leaders must preserve its independence and unity by not permitting it to become identified with particular programmes or class interests. The church is here essentially transcendent and above the world of political struggle, a definition which must rule out the suggestion that any internal divisions might be caused by 'class conflict'. The bishops' position appeared to reflect that taken by the united Latin American episcopate at Puebla where it affirmed that 'Party politics is properly the realm of lay people . . . Pastors, on the other hand, must be concerned with unity.' However, since Puebla also restated Medellín's option for the poor, the question is raised whether the bishops did not leave the church in a somewhat ambiguous position. It was to remain committed to the liberation of the poor, but at the same time avoid identification with specific political programmes or movements which aimed to achieve that liberation.

The way in which, for church leaders, perceptions of the church can profoundly affect political responses has been emphasized by recent sociological study. On the basis of extensive research into the church in Venezuela and Colombia, Daniel Levine has argued that although the way in which church leaders see social and political problems plays a major role in shaping their actions,

> for religious people, political responses are mediated through a set of self-images and role definitions which shape what they think they ought to do, as members of a transcendent Church, regardless of what the temporal challenges or problems are seen to be . . . Visions of the institution . . . provide conceptual and behavioural frameworks for action . . .[20]

Among the bishops and radicals in Nicaragua different 'visions of the institution' clearly played a major role in shaping their respective political positions, and may offer a second explanation for the differing stances toward the revolution found within the church.

The church's response to the challenge of a revolutionary situation was mixed. Whilst some Christians saw their presence in the process in terms of the church making effective its preference for the poor, and found that they were led into a new and deeper religious commitment, others became involved only when they felt circumstances left them no other option. From others still, including most of the hierarchy, there was no unequivocal sign of support for the revolution until the transfer of power was virtually completed. These disparate responses inevitably led to tensions within the church and the revolution at large which, although they became submerged in the months immediately following the insurrection, were to cause severe problems as the task of consolidating the revolution got under way.

3 · By Schisms Rent Asunder

On 17 November 1979, four months after the insurrection, the Catholic bishops issued a pastoral letter expressing their strong support for the revolution. They acknowledged what they called 'the present revolutionary moment' to be 'an opportune time truly to implement the church's option for the poor', and declared that the basis of their commitment to the process was a desire to build the kingdom of God, a kingdom of liberation, justice and life. In a lengthy section they spoke approvingly of Nicaragua's movement towards socialism – provided that it ensured that the interests of the majority of citizens remained paramount – and in a significant shift from their pre-revolutionary stance acknowledged the role of the FSLN at the head of the forces which contributed to the revolution.

The bishops continued to express their approval of the revolution until well into the following year. They compared the Literacy Crusade, which began in March, to the work of 'Christ the Teacher', and on a visit to Cuba before Easter Archbishop Obando y Bravo affirmed his belief that the Sandinista revolution was seeking the good of the majority. For the first ten months of the revolution the church made a united response to the situation. By May, however, the honeymoon period was over, and by October it was hard to believe there had been any relationship at all between some sections of the church and the revolution.

Somewhat unsurprisingly the cracks in the church after the revolution appeared in similar places to those which had developed before, and in a broad sense there was some correlation between a degree of commitment to build the revolution and a willingness to consolidate it. Among the CEBs and many religious communities

30

there was widespread support for and involvement in revolutionary projects like the National Crusade for Literacy and the Popular Health Campaigns. Three priests who had long-standing connections with the Sandinistas, Miguel D'Escoto and Fernando and Ernesto Cardenal, accepted senior positions in the Government of National Reconstruction, and a number of other priests and religious accepted posts in government and Sandinista organizations like the Defence Committees (CDS) and Rural Workers' Association (ATC). The bishops, however, began to distance themselves from the revolution within the first year, the turning point being a communiqué in May 1980 calling for the priests in the government to resign and be replaced by lay-people. By October, less than a year after their declaration of support, the bishops' criticisms of the Sandinista administration had become much more overt, and a statement issued that month denounced in strong terms many aspects of the revolution. Writing in the wake of an official FSLN policy statement on religion they spoke of Nicaragua's 'search for its historic liberation, not . . . for a new Pharaoh', and criticized the FSLN for *inter alia* limiting democracy, attempting to divide the church, and restricting its sphere of influence. 'Neither the church nor the Christians oppose the revolution,' they wrote, 'but oppose those who transform it ideologically against the religious spirit of our people.'

From this point on the hierarchy's attitude to the Sandinista government and the priests serving in it continued to harden. In their letter of Easter 1984 they made some outspoken criticism of post-revolutionary developments in Nicaragua and referred, in the context of a discussion on sin, to a materialistic and atheistic educational system, a use of the mass media to encourage a spirit of violence, and the suffering of peasants and Indians who had been forced to abandon their homes in a futile search for peace (a reference to the Miskito relocation carried out by the Sandinistas in 1982).[1] They noted that there was effectively a civil war in the country, and spoke of the need for reconciliation through dialogue involving all citizens, including those who had taken up arms against their government. This was clearly a reference to the counter-revolutionary or *contra*[2] forces which, with the backing of the Reagan administration in Washington, had been waging a war on the Sandinista government since the early 1980s. The bishops, by

31

referring to a 'war between Nicaraguans' and the dishonesty of blaming internal aggression on foreign aggression, understood the attacks on the government to be entirely the work of Nicaraguans disaffected with the régime.

In their Easter 1986 letter the bishops again spoke of a war situation in the country, though they appeared less tolerant than before of the *contras*' position.[3] They urged resistance to all foreign ideologies and pressures, and denounced in an unspecific way foreign forces which were taking advantage of the situation to promote economic and ideological exploitation. They condemned any form of aid, whatever its source, 'if it is the cause of destruction, pain or death for our families or of hatred among Nicaraguans'. Whilst their criticisms of the Sandinista government were considerably more muted in this letter, the bishops did make a passing reference to the 'scandalous disobedience of some ecclesiastics', which was intended, no doubt, to encompass the priests serving in the government. They also made a lengthy attack on the subversive and divisive tendencies of the 'popular church', among whose members they discerned a certain sympathy with Marxism.

How might the bishops' apparent change of stance towards the revolution be accounted for? For some critics the question does not really arise since the bishops, having not supported the Sandinistas before the revolution, might therefore not be expected to do so afterwards. Like the middle-class opposition, their support for the revolution owed its origins more to a dislike of Somoza than a commitment to the Sandinistas, and therefore some falling away among their ranks was only to be expected. But if the bishops' November 1979 letter did reflect a genuine and new-found commitment to the revolutionary process, then a major shift in their position had occurred, and their subsequent departure from it merits further investigation.

Perhaps the most plausible explanation for the bishops' withdrawal of support is that in the months immediately following the insurrection it was still unclear, at least to some, which direction the revolution would eventually take, and it was therefore possible for different groups within the country, using the same terminology, to hold varying ideas about where the process was heading. That this was to some extent true of the bishops may be seen from their letters of the period. In November 1979, in addition to giving a detailed blueprint of the form of socialism that they would find acceptable, they spoke also of their confidence that the revolutionary process would be something original and creative, resulting in a society 'fully and authentically Nicaraguan, neither capitalistic, nor dependent, nor totalitarian'. In an earlier letter, written just twelve days after the insurrection, they also showed their belief in the openness of the process by speaking of 'the revolutionary projects that everyone wants', 'serious confusions both in ideological aspects and in the organization of new state structures', and the need to 'remain free . . . *vis-à-vis* any system to opt always for people'.

Yet the crucial decision which faced the bishops, and indeed the whole church, did not concern the type of society they wished to construct in some hypothetical post-revolutionary situation, but whether or not to identify with the actual historical process going on around them, a popular Sandinista-led revolution. Despite its important contribution the church could not claim the revolution as its own, nor the sole right to govern its course, and it would appear that when the full implications of this were realized, i.e. that henceforth the church as an institution would have less influence and status than under Somoza and colonial rule, the bishops reacted against the revolutionary process and withdrew their support for it. Whilst many Catholics believed that the new situation offered the church an opportunity to break its traditional links with power, the bishops appeared uneasy about accepting the full implications of this. Among those Christians who did want this break, however, commitment to the revolutionary process deepened, and thus at an early stage were sown the seeds of division within the church which were in due course to produce a very bitter crop.

In seeking explanations for the diversity of attitudes within the church, socio-economic factors again appear material. For many Nicaraguans the revolution meant a significant improvement in their quality of life: the literacy rate rose from fifty per cent to over eighty per cent, health campaigns eradicated or controlled many common diseases, infant mortality declined, and large areas of land were handed over to peasant farmers and co-operatives. Clearly those who benefited from these improvements, particularly the poor, were inclined to give the revolution and the Sandinistas enthusiastic support, whilst those for whom the revolution meant some loss of power, wealth or status, notably the middle and upper classes, tended to be critical of it or even hostile towards it. And as before the revolution, similarities in response between the Catholic hierarchy and this latter sector are identifiable. The call for the priests in the government to resign, for example, which was the first public sign of the bishops' withdrawal of support for the revolution, came within a month of a similar sign by the bourgeoisie in the form of the resignation from the Council of State of the industrialist Alfonso Robelo. One explanation for this similarity might be that both had expected to continue playing a major role in society after the revolution, and were unwilling to accept a less influential position in the new order. Thus Miguel D'Escoto could write in 1981 that 'there are cases in which the church echoes all the fears and lamentations of the bourgeoisie as their privileges are affected by the victorious popular processes'.[4] Fernando Cardenal also suggests that the opposition of the church and the industrial sector were connected: the rich, he argues, gave their support because they wanted a change in figureheads rather than a change of system, and so when the Sandinistas began implementing economic reforms they became opposed to the revolution. 'Unfortunately,' he concludes, 'religious elements have also sounded an echo . . . of sorrow and protest of those who are pining for their privileges . . .'[5]

Another possible explanation for the bishops' change of stance since November 1979 may be discovered by examining the changing composition of the hierarchy and ascertaining the individual position of each bishop and the degree of influence each exercises. Such an investigation would reveal, for example, that one bishop believed to be sympathetic to the FSLN had to spend a good deal of time since the revolution out of the country receiving medical treatment. A comparison of the signatures on the November 1979 letter (which was supportive of the revolution) with those under the more hostile letter of April 1984 reveals that although six bishops signed both, a seventh signatory to the first letter had been replaced, and two other prelates added to the episcopate, by 1984. However, since it is believed that at least two of these new bishops were broadly sympathetic to the government, an explanation based on changes in personnel is unlikely to prove adequate in itself. Informed observers in fact maintain that of the ten bishops perhaps only four are strongly opposed to the Sandinistas, with four others open to dialogue and two uncommitted. If this is the case, then factors like the influence of individual bishops and the nature of the issue at hand may well be the most important in determining their collective response. On certain occasions when a statement from the bishops might have been expected but failed to appear, the reason may have been an inability to reach a consensus position.

It is doubtful whether the bishops would agree that the position they have adopted since their November 1979 letter does represent any change of stance from the one they held at that time. Their view would be that they have remained faithful to their commitment to a society not dependent or totalitarian, while the revolutionary government, by accepting Cuban and Soviet economic and military aid and by imposing a state of emergency on at least two occasions, has created a society which is just that. They would claim to have maintained, as they did under Somoza, an independently critical stance towards the government with the freedom, as before, to praise what is good and condemn what is evil. This position, they would argue, is much to be preferred to that of the priests in the government, whose identification with the Sandinistas is so complete that it has robbed them of their liberty to engage in prophetic denunciation of any aspects of government policy which may be manifestly un-Christian.

The significance of the bishops' opposition to the government should not be underestimated, for they have effectively emerged as the main focus for all political dissent in Nicaragua. Whilst some observers argue that they have been instrumentalized by the opposition, or have been willing to collaborate with any groups intent on overthrowing the Sandinistas, it is probably as much by default as by conscious effort that they find themselves co-ordinating the anti-government movement. The political opposition to the Sandinistas is recognized as being organizationally weak, and lacking in any outstanding national leaders, and therefore the church, as a traditionally powerful and influential force in the land, has been well-placed to act as an umbrella for disaffected groups.

Some observers have also suggested that the bishops' stance since the early 1980s has led to their being identified, not only with the indigenous opposition groups, but with the United States government. The Antonio Valdivieso Centre (CAV), a radical ecumenical body responsible for training CEB leaders, has been strongly critical of the bishops for describing the conflict in Nicaragua as internal and not denouncing it as:

a war that the Reagan administration is directing and financing against our country from Honduras and Costa Rica through the use of the old national guard of Somoza and mercenaries from other countries . . . the Bishops lend support to President Reagan's policy, by upholding his claim that the war in Nicaragua is an internal conflict . . .[6]

The fact that Nicaraguans have requested and received weapons from their own government to defend themselves from the *contras* has also provoked criticism of the bishops' assertion that what is taking place in the country is a civil war. Fernando Cardenal has also criticized the timing of the bishops' call for him to leave the government, noting that it came when the country was in a state of general alert, 'when my people is in critical danger, calumniated and accosted by the most powerful country in the world'.[7]

Other more positive connections between the bishops and foreign opponents of the revolution have also been alleged. In 1984 reports in two United States newspapers, the *New York Times* and the *National Catholic Reporter*, suggested that Archbishop Obando y Bravo had been negotiating with a known CIA agent for financial help to oppose the Sandinista régime. Similar allegations appeared in two Mexican papers. According to the *National Catholic Reporter* the Archbishop said he had been 'working on a "development plan" to thwart the Marxist-Leninist policies of the Sandinistas'.[8] Political significance was also inferred from the Archbishop's decision to celebrate his first mass after elevation to cardinal in April 1985 in Miami with *contra* leaders present. However, Cardinal Obando has described as 'slander' accusations that he or other bishops have used their visits to the United States to solicit aid for *contra* groups, and Archbishop O'Connor of New York, who visited Nicaragua in March 1985 with a delegation of US bishops, said on his return that 'not a single bishop asked our support in encouraging financial and military assistance for the *contras*'.[9]

Whilst the bishops might be criticized for allowing political rather than pastoral concerns to shape their response to the revolutionary government, similar accusations have also been levelled at priests and lay-people supportive of the new order. One leading critic of the Sandinista régime, Humberto Belli, has spoken of revolutionary Christians who, following the liberation theology priority of praxis before reflection, have claimed that 'revolutionary commitment should not be judged from the standpoint of the Gospel but the other way around'. He notes that Christian belief has become so identified with revolutionary praxis that commitment to the FSLN is now the most important criterion for distinguishing between real Christians and those who are 'just reactionaries dressed up in religious garb'. According to Belli 'pro-Marxist Christians' have encouraged a shift in loyalties among believers by demanding they give their unconditional support to the revolution and not to the church.[10] In a similar vein the bishops have spoken of a small part of the church which has submitted itself to the influence of a materialistic ideology. Identifying this 'belligerent group of priests, men and women religious, and laity of different nationalities' by the term 'popular church' they have accused them of reinterpreting and rewriting the Word of God to make it fit their own ideology, and of attempting to divide the church 'by giving rise to "class struggle" within its ranks according to the Marxist ideology'. Another leading church official, Mgr Bismark Carballo, has spoken of the 'popular church' making a breach for Marxism to enter Latin America through the churches. The bishops have also suggested that the priests involved in the government have been instrumentalized by the Sandinistas in the same way that totalitarian systems try to justify themselves by soliciting the support of the church – a similar accusation to that which critics have levelled at the bishops themselves in respect of their relationship with the conservative opposition.

One point of interest about this conflict is that although it is at root political, concerning attitudes toward the Sandinista government, it has been conducted to a large extent as though it were primarily religious. In fact the struggle by different political factions to win popular support has often assumed the appearance of a contest for religious loyalties. One reason might be that both sides want to imply they have divine sanction for their respective positions and that they are speaking prophetically, and so present essentially political arguments within a theological framework. Thus as before the revolution the bishops endorsed armed resistance to the state by reference to the traditional doctrine of the just insurrection, so their subsequent criticism of the revolution has been placed within discourses on sin, confession and the need for conversion. In a similar vein the priests in the Sandinista government have continued to speak of their political involvement in terms of obedience to the call of God. A second reason might be that neither the conservative opposition nor the Catholic hierarchy has felt able to advocate openly a return to the pre-revolutionary social order, with a concomitant restoration of their former privileges, and so engage in their ideological struggle against the FSLN by using religious arguments to arouse opposition to the existing régime. If this policy has been adopted by middle-class groups then a further reason for the church's emergence as a focus of political opposition suggests itself, namely its ability to offer to such groups, as Luis Serra puts it, 'the angelical disguise of religion with which to conceal their class interests'.[11]

Underlying both these points is the tremendous influence which religion has in Nicaragua, both on individuals and communities. As a means of giving legitimacy or appeal to a political position it can be a vital tool in any debate, as both the FSLN and their opponents recognize. In a speech at a May Day rally in 1984, for example, Jaime Wheelock of the FSLN directorate suggested not only that the Front was being faithful to Christian principles, but that the revolution was fulfilling scripture. 'Who said, "Blessed be the poor for they shall inherit the earth"?', he asked the crowd, who, despite the transposition of beautitudes, gave him the answer he wanted. 'And who is giving land to the poor here? Who took land away from the *somocistas* and the rich to give it to the poor?'; to which came the anticipated reply 'The revolution!'[12] In an interview a year earlier Wheelock consciously used Christian symbolism to emphasize *sandinismo*'s fidelity to the faith. We go beyond the ideals of Christianity, he said, 'because we are prepared to shed our last drop of blood for you'. Recalling two heroes of the revolutionary struggle, he spoke of Carlos Fonseca who 'fell and shed his blood for the Nicaraguan people', and Edgard Lang who 'fought for a higher purpose – to die and give his life for the people'.[13] In a May Day speech in 1982 Tomás Borge, in a eulogy to fellow FSLN co-founder Fonseca, spoke of 'your working class . . . which will be faithful to you until victory, until blood, until death . . . We are the gatherers of your resurrection'.[14] Borge has also spoken of archaeologists finding the supposed tomb of Sandino 'empty', and phrases like 'Sandino lives' and 'Sandino yesterday, Sandino today, Sandino for ever' have become common in Nicaragua. Within the church some clergy sympathetic to the revolution have also begun to give new meaning to traditional religious symbols and concepts. Attempts have been made, for example, to find a new image for the Virgin Mary, who has had a profound influence on Nicaraguan women by promoting motherhood and virginity as ideal states and encouraging submissiveness, self-denial and a sense of inferiority. Now she is sometimes represented more as a champion and liberator of the oppressed than a figure of passivity and obedience, a role reflected in such slogans as, 'With the Virgin Mary on our side, we'll smash the bourgeoisie!'

Examples abound, too, of ways in which groups opposed to the Sandinistas have also used Christian symbolism for political effect. In December 1981 some interpreted the miracle of a weeping statue of Mary (later exposed as a hoax) as a lament for a Nicaragua that was going astray. The floods the following year were proclaimed by some Christians to be a punishment from God for the 'Communist direction' of the government, and a Protestant evangelist announced that he was coming to Nicaragua 'to help in the great and urgent task of annulling the satanical work which is palpable in that nation'. This somewhat incautious statement cost him his entry into the country. A more subtle example of an apparently orthodox use of Christian doctrine to convey an ideological message occurred during a large evangelistic campaign in Managua in 1984, organized by Protestants uncommitted to the revolution. At one point in his address the preacher declared that the answer to the world's problems was not to be found in Moscow, Havana or Washington: 'Jesus Christ is the only one who can change your life and give you freedom!' Parallel examples have been observed at Catholic masses where the words 'This is the *only Lord* of the Nicaraguans' may be repeated several times at the elevation of the host. *Contra* groups have also used religious symbols to try to gain support for their campaign, sometimes leaving holy images behind in the wake of their attacks. A witness to one such attack reported that after leaving some lighted candles, an image of Mary, and a picture of Christ in a chapel, the *contras* shouted out that they were fighting a 'holy war' against Communism and that God was with them. 'Simple people like the *campesinos* are very religious and become confused by all of this,' the witness said.[15] The approach in which God and patriotism are placed in contraposition to Communism and atheism, as representations of 'good' and 'evil', is widely used by groups opposed to the

Sandinistas to undermine support for the government and the revolution.

As before the revolution, the political differences within the Catholic church have been reinforced by a fundamental disagreement over the place and role of the church in a revolutionary situation. Similar models continue to define the debate – a horizontal church identified with the poor and a traditional hierarchical church under episcopal authority – but in the changed political and social environment since the revolution this disagreement has assumed a greater significance. The central question in the debate is whether the new social and political order created by the revolution also prescribes a new role for the church, and at least three factors suggest that it does. The first is a conviction that, unlike *somocismo*, the revolution is legitimate in itself and does not need to ask the church for any additional sacralization. Fernando Cardenal sees this legitimacy stemming from 'the search for justice and liberation of the exploited . . . its consistency with the gospel'.[16] Clearly, ethical criteria are important, though widespread support for the revolution might be considered a more objective basis for determining its legitimacy, certainly relative to *somocismo*. A second factor is that the new society created by the revolution has allowed less space than before for religion. This has not arisen through any conscious attack on religion by the FSLN but because, through its role in leading the revolution, reinforced by a convincing victory in the subsequent elections, the Front has come to provide direction and meaning for many people, formerly the exclusive prerogative of the church. Since the revolution there has also been less scope for social and charitable activity by the church because the state has assumed a greater responsibility for areas like education, development and welfare. A third factor is the observable erosion of traditional religiosity that has occurred since the revolution. Again this is not necessarily the result of state hostility to religion, but a consequence of the people having become, through their participation in the revolutionary process, agents of their own destiny.

Those sympathetic to the revolution argue that, in offering the church a new role in society, the process also gives it the opportunity to make a complete break with its past. Fernando Cardenal, for example, describes his presence within the Sandinista government as 'a symbol of the rupture with power in the church' and 'a clear sign of a church in solidarity with the cause of the poor'.[17] The basis of the church's relationship with the revolutionary government is very different from that which underlay its earlier alliances with the colonial powers and *somocismo*. 'Our new project did not mean participating in power,' Cardenal has written, 'but in reinforcing the possibility that the poor would have the power.'[18] Miguel D'Escoto has also spelt out what the church's mission should be in a revolutionary situation – a concern for the people for whom Christ suffered, died and rose again. 'I don't think the church needs to go looking for privileges and extraordinary rights in order to accomplish its mission,' he has written. 'Its mission is not to be concerned for itself, but to be consistent with the faith . . .'[19]

The argument that post-revolutionary society suggests a completely changed role for the church is further strengthened by the fact that the state does not in any case offer it a relationship on the same basis as under the old order. Scope for the traditional Christendom model of church-state relations no longer exists. What does remain open to the church, as D'Escoto implies, is the possibility of mission. As the Belgian sociologist François Houtart has observed,

> though there is less space today for the traditional Nicaraguan institutional church, paradoxically there is more space for evangelization carried out in depth.[20]

It is important to note that evangelization in this context is often very broadly defined and encompasses not merely spiritual conversion but, in line with the new emphasis suggested by liberation theology, a practical commitment to the cause of the poor and the consolidation of the revolution. As one evangelical writer has put it, evangelism is done,

> with a daily testimony, with constant praxis, with deeds, not words . . . to evangelize means to suffer with those who suffer, to weep with those who weep, to accompany the people in harvesting coffee and cotton, to comfort the young people in their struggle to block the return of the sin of *somocismo*.[21]

Evangelism of this sort was, according to Fernando Cardenal, essential for priests like himself who had a duty to ensure that Christian values remained present in the process. The diocesan committee in Estelí also commented that 'Christians must be present in the process if they wish to preserve the Christian dimension of the revolution'.[22] A Christian presence is not uncritical and recognizes that within the process there is sin which has to be redeemed, but since the gospel demonstrates that redemption can only be accomplished by incarnation so, it is argued, the church can only influence the revolution by being fully identified with it.

Among the bishops this new model of a missionary church has not been widely accepted, and they appear to have remained committed to defending the church's traditional position in society, despite the transformation that society has undergone. To some critics this tendency not to accept a new role for the church in the post-revolutionary situation is at the root of the bishops' hostility to the Sandinista government. Their continued adherence to the idea of a paternalistic church arises, it is argued, from an unwillingness to accept that the Sandinista government has been recognized by the people as an alternative source of moral authority. Perhaps it is also significant that the bishops' first overt criticism of the government came shortly after the promulgation of its official statement on religion. It is not unlikely that the document's reference to the revolutionary state having a secular basis, and its definition of religion as a personal matter, were perceived by the bishops as an insult to the church's commitment to the revolution and a threat to the traditional authority of the church. Yet the main reason for the bishops' commitment to a traditional model may well be a fear that the revolutionary process will eventually bring about some sort of split in the church which would undermine their position. In recent years they have expressed deep concerns about another church establishing itself outside or even upon the ruins of the constitutional church. In 1984 they spoke of a small part of the church which had 'abandoned ecclesial unity', and which was 'sowing confusion (by) extolling its own ideas and slandering the legitimate pastors', and in their Easter 1986 letter sharply attacked what they called the 'popular church' for actively undermining the foundations upon which the unity of the Catholic church is built. A reassertion of their traditional authority may therefore be seen by the bishops as the most effective way to discourage this tendency. The Pope has shared the bishops' concerns about disunity and in his letters and messages to the Nicaraguan church has focused much of his attention on the threat posed to it by 'parallel magisteriums'. His response has also been to spell out where authority lies in the church and stress repeatedly the need for unity around the bishops. 'I pray that you may be able to ensure that the Christians of your country will not be divided because of opposing ideologies,' he wrote to the bishops in 1982, ' . . . the unity of the faithful must be concretely woven around the bishop . . . Without him this unity does not exist or is falsified.'

How far these moves to reassert the bishops' authority will be successful is open to question. The experience of participating in the revolution and gaining a greater share of power has changed the perception of the church among many Catholics. Many now have the benefit of education and an improved standard of living and have less reason to look to the church for security and support in the face of poverty and exploitation. Many have also found that since the revolution they have been able to have a greater say in the decisions that affect their lives, for example at work and in the community, and this may have left them unimpressed by the bishops' renewed emphasis on their traditional authority and their calls for the faithful to fall into line behind them. More fundamentally the so-called *iglesia popular* – which is not to be confused with the CEBs, though they are one manifestation of it – has challenged the traditional bases of authority and unity within the church. The experience of participating in a revolution, together with the influence of liberation theology, has led many to see Christian unity embodied in a shared commitment to the poor, rather than as something to be built around the traditional authority of the bishops, and authority emanating out of an identification with the people and a commitment to consolidate the revolution. Hierarchical authority has become an increasingly foreign concept among many Catholics radicalized by the revolution, and many have tended to bypass it altogether. The bishops' fears about a split are therefore not without foundation, though for their part the base communities have affirmed their commitment to work for unity in the church and have denied that any 'popular church' exists outside the mainstream of the church. They argue that the communities, with their emphasis on lay participation and initiative, were actually encouraged by the official church at Medellín and Puebla (and Vatican II), and have been the means of changing and transforming the church from within – a process which does involve analysis and criticism of the church, they admit, but not a questioning of the fundamental authority of the bishops. Whether the church is eventually rent asunder or not, the political differences that have arisen in it have created a crisis of authority with potentially far-reaching consequences.

One final question to consider is what effect this intra-church conflict might have on the country's religious life. One radical outcome might be the disappearance of the church altogether, not in the wake of persecution or hostility from the state, but as a direct consequence of the new praxis-centred theology adopted by revolutionary Christians. For these Christians the faith is best expressed through a practical commitment to feed the hungry, clothe the naked and heal the sick by consolidating the revolution, and as Luis Serra has suggested,

> this type of religious practice calls into question the need for a religious institution which administers and monopolizes religious services and which develops a specific space for religious practice.[23]

Another possibility, already hinted at, is that as attitudes towards the revolution continue to polarize, a complete split in the church may occur. In 1984 César Jerez described this polarization as having reached 'unparalleled levels of visciousness',[24] and events in subsequent years have not encouraged the belief that either side has become more restrained in its criticism of the other. Accusations of heresy have been directed against those firmly committed to the revolution, and Cardinal Obando has been accused of committing a greater sin than any covered by canon law for apparently refusing to condemn the *contras*. Even if there is a concern for unity among those Catholics committed to furthering the revolution, for many the bishops' antipathy towards the government has posed a profound dilemma. It is not the spiritual authority of the bishops which has been questioned but the political direction in which they appear to want to lead the church, and it is resistance to this which may ultimately bring about a division in the church.

Even if a split were not to occur, the church is clearly being weakened by its internal divisions. The disaffection which some Catholics have for their church's official position has led to a steady decline in church attendance and participation, a tendency particularly noticeable among the young. The significance of this in the long term is enormous given the fact that over two-thirds of the population is under twenty-four years of age. For Nicaraguans, religion has traditionally been identified with the church as an institution, and so when that institution projects a negative image, as some perceive it has done since the revolution, an indifference to religion in any form is a likely outcome.

Faced with what they perceive to be a choice between the revolution and the church, some Christians have also opted out of the latter to channel their revolutionary commitment through the FSLN. Among them have been some Delegates of the Word who have given up their ministry to work in Sandinista organizations such as the Rural Workers' Association (ATC) and the Sandinista Defence Committees (CDS). This development has been more common in areas where church influence was weak and where the functions it previously exercised have been taken over by the government. An FSLN policy of recruiting such people has also encouraged this process, and it is interesting to speculate how far this may be linked to a perception among leading Sandinistas that there is a threat to its hegemony in the revolution from the CEBs. It is possible that the FSLN's attempt to define religion as a private matter may not have arisen solely from a desire to limit the influence of the institutional church *vis-à-vis* its own, but also from a concern that the grassroots CEBs could become an alternative source of moral authority for the masses. Allegations have been made that the Sandinistas actually recruited priests sympathetic to liberation theology as a precaution against that theology becoming a recognized alternative to their own ideology.[25] The Front may also have feared that if the influence of the institutional church declined in the light of its anti-revolutionary stance, and support for the 'popular church' grew, that church might threaten its own power structures in addition to those of the institutional church. It would also be interesting to ascertain the attitude of the priests in the government to the Sandinista policy on religion, since their testimonies suggest they would be most firmly opposed to any form of 'privatized' religion and unalarmed about the increasing influence of the 'popular church'.

François Houtart has offered a further reason why the failure of the church as an institution to respond to the new revolutionary situation might lead to a general weakening or loss of faith throughout society. The nub of his argument is that, since all theological representations are culturally conditioned, in a period of radical social, economic or intellectual change new representations are necessary in order to keep faith from disappearing. If, for example, in a new socio-cultural context new ways of representing the relationship between God and humanity are not discovered, then there is a danger that the very idea of such a relationship will be abandoned altogether. Where changes in the social relations of production have been brought about by the mass of the people themselves then, says Houtart,

> a certain representation of God as the direct author of that society and social order no longer functions. Such a representation loses its credibility when the common people become historical agents of their destiny. If new religious representations adequate for the new degree of development are not then drawn up, there is a danger that religious faith will disappear.[26]

The question therefore really becomes not whether religion can survive in a revolutionary situation but what form any surviving religion will take, and for radical theologians only a theology which takes into account the new economic and cultural environment and the needs of the 'new person' who helped to create it will make any headway in that new context.

Despite a rapid change in the social order new representations are unlikely to be assimilated quickly. The attempt to make the image of the Virgin Mary more appropriate to the revolutionary struggle is a case in point, and commenting on this Jane Deighton *et al* have observed that,

> for the Virgin to be a true model for the 'new woman' would require a complete clearing away of centuries of misogynistic church prejudice, a tradition that affirms women's subordination to men and which the figure of the Virgin is instrumental in maintaining.[27]

The responsibility for religious reconstruction, and therefore for maintaining the faith rests, claims Houtart, with the institutional church rather than the people themselves. In Nicaragua, he considers, the bishops must either adopt a new definition of the faith to correspond to the new situation, or risk the emergence either of a very superficial faith or the abandonment, particularly by the young, of a traditional religion which has failed to maintain any meaning in the new socio-political context. Critics have also warned the bishops that they risk further isolation from the people if they fail to recognize how the experience of revolution has given many a new understanding of what it is to be the church. And for D'Escoto there will be a further consequence if the new self-identification the people have gained since the revolution is ignored:

> If the proclamation of the Christian message does not take into account this increasing maturity, it will be reduced to the restricted area of a private concern. It will remain on the fringe of history.[28]

Clearly, however, if the bishops are committed to halting the revolutionary process and restoring something like the previous order such concerns will not, for them, appear so pressing.

4 · A State of Tension

The bishops' interpretation of a number of incidents since the revolution has led them increasingly to accuse the government of systematically persecuting the church and attempting to undermine the faith of the people through a programme of indoctrination. A consideration of some of these incidents may help to identify the roots of this tension and the power struggle that has developed between the government and the Catholic hierarchy.

Censorship

One charge frequently laid by the bishops at the door of the government is that of suppression and censorship of official church documents and broadcasts. Two letters from the Pope to the Nicaraguan hierarchy, one written in 1982 the other in 1985, were both initially withheld by the government. The first, which was dated 29 June but not circulated until 8 August, spoke of the need for church unity to be built around the bishops, and the official Sandinista explanation for the delay in its publication was its openness to manipulation for political ends – the bishops were by then recognized opponents of the government – and its timing – it arrived around the time of a *contra* attack on San Francisco del Norte in which fifteen Nicaraguans were killed and eight taken hostage. The tenor of the second letter, in which the Pope spoke of the painful situation the church had endured for so long, 'suffering privation, grief and uncertainty', also laid it open to interpretation by those opposed to the government of papal support for their position. It was originally severely cut by the censors but, like the earlier letter, later published in full. To the bishops the suppression of the letters appeared, no doubt, to be an unwarranted interference in church affairs, although the government considered both politically controversial and potentially subversive.

The church has also complained of censorship of its radio station Radio Católica. In 1981 some restrictions were imposed on its programmes, and in 1986, following its failure to broadcast a speech by President Daniel Ortega, it was closed down altogether. Also in 1981 Archbishop Obando's weekly televised sermon on the Sandinista network was discontinued. The government originally asked the archbishop to share his slot with other preachers, offering to retain him on a monthly basis, but this proved unacceptable and, in the ensuing stalemate, the broadcasts stopped altogether. To the church this clearly appeared to be a basic denial of its liberty to reach its flock via the mass media, although the government, whilst it may have genuinely wanted to vary the programme's format, was no doubt anxious to remove what it saw as an important platform for the political opposition.

The bishops claimed that the restrictions placed upon them were even more severe after the state of emergency imposed in October 1985. The government defended the measure as essential in view of the external threats to the country, and priests sympathetic to the government maintained that it did not materially affect their way of life nor entail any loss of religious freedom. It was less severe than those imposed before, they claimed, and had not led to a restoration of the death penalty, martial law, curfews or restrictions on movement outside areas of conflict. To the church hierarchy, however, it represented one more step towards silencing the church and the government's ultimate goal of establishing a totalitarian Marxist-Leninist state. In mid-1986 the opposition newspaper *La Prensa*, which had operated subject to some censorship since the revolution, was closed down.

Harassment

As well as censorship of its broadcasts and publications, the bishops have also cited many examples of attacks by Sandinistas on church officials and property. In 1984 ten foreign priests – four Spaniards, two Costa Ricans, two Italians, a Canadian and a Panamanian – were expelled by the government, some after more than thirty years' residence in the country. During the 1985 state of emergency a number of priests and lay Catholic activists were detained, and on one occasion thirty foreign priests were summoned to the security headquarters in Managua and threatened with deportation. A further seventeen were denied visas. In October 1985 government forces occupied the offices of a Catholic social agency and seized the first issue of the magazine *Iglesia*. The following June the offices were handed back, but in the meantime furniture and equipment had been removed, together with the press used to print the magazine. In July 1986 Bishop Pablo Antonio Vega, the second most senior figure in the hierarchy, was denied permission to re-enter the country after a visit abroad. To the bishops these incidents and others provide clear evidence of an anti-clerical strain within *sandinismo*, and a commitment by the government gradually to reduce the influence of the Catholic church in the country. The government, however, has justified its action in each case on political or legal rather than religious grounds. It claimed that all the priests who were deported or detained had been involved in unlawful or anti-government activity and were therefore to be treated like any other foreign nationals found guilty of such offences. Many of the indigenous clergy who were arrested were also charged with unlawful conduct. Bishop Vega was an outspoken critic of the Sandinista government, and was reported to have said shortly before his expulsion that the decision of the US Congress to give aid to the *contras* was legitimate and valid. The official reason for the confiscation of *Iglesia* was the failure of the Archbishop's press office to complete the necessary legal registration requirements, although the inclusion of an article critical of the government's conscription policy in its first issue no doubt also made a clamp-down more attractive.

Pro-government Christians have also pointed out that harassment of church-people has not been confined to the government, since the church hierarchy itself has also attempted from time to time to transfer or expel clergy known to be sympathetic to the government. In January 1986 Fr Uriel Molina, a parish priest in Managua and director of the Antonio Valdivieso Centre (CAV), claimed that because of his support for the government he had been asked by his superiors to leave the country for a year. He was subsequently allowed to stay, although a number of other priests and religious, whom the church sees as rebellious, have been transferred either within or out of the country.

The bishops have also complained about attempts by the Sandinistas to incriminate individual priests, the most celebrated case being that involving Mgr Bismark Carballo, the director of Radio Católica and press secretary and official spokesperson for the Archbishop. In August 1982 pictures of Fr Carballo *déshabillé* appeared in the national press and on the government television network. According to the police version, a television crew filming a demonstration in Managua was suddenly distracted by the sound of gunfire and the sight of an unclothed man running down the street pursued by an armed assailant. They filmed the incident although unaware at the time of the identity of the man. The police, who were also accompanying the demonstration, took both men away for questioning, and the assailant maintained that on returning to his home he had found Carballo in bed with his wife and had decided to seek revenge. In an interview she later gave to a pro-government newspaper the woman alleged she had had a lengthy affair with the priest. Carballo's version was that he was having lunch with the woman, a regular member of his congregation, when an armed man entered the house and forced him to undress. The man then made him leave the house in full view of a crowd which had gathered outside and which happened to contain reporters and a camera crew from the Sandinista media. The whole incident, he maintained, was a plan to embarrass the church. Although subsequent claims and counter-claims gradually drew a veil of ambiguity over the affair, Carballo himself became a figurehead for anti-revolutionary sections of the church who held masses to repair the dishonour done to him and regarded him as a victim of a Sandinista attempt to undermine the church. If there had been this intention on the government's part it to some extent backfired, since a widespread concern about the disrespect shown to the priest by the circulation of the photographs led the government to admit it had erred in publicizing the story, though it still maintained the truth of its account. Mgr Carballo was also the target of apparent further government harassment in June 1986 when he was refused permission to board his connecting flight home from Miami after attending a peace conference in Paris. This was a few days before the expulsion of Bishop Vega.

In June 1984 a parish priest in Managua, Fr Amado Peña, was at the centre of another controversy following the broadcast of a film which appeared to show him handling arms for the *contras*. Peña, who was noted as an outspoken critic of the government, had been filmed leaving a car to pass a bag containing hand grenades, explosives and a *contra* flag to a man in another car. The government news media denounced the priest as a terrorist accomplice and charges were brought against him, although the case was never heard and the charges later dropped. After reviewing the case Amnesty International considered Peña to have been falsely implicated in criminal activity.[1] It was following protests about the government's treatment of Fr Peña that the ten foreign priests were deported later in 1984.

Human rights

In February 1982 the bishops issued a statement criticizing the Sandinista government for forcibly removing many thousands of Miskito Indians from their homeland on the Honduran border and destroying their houses and property. The bishops condemned the harshness of the move and spoke of a violation of human rights. The Sandinistas defended their action on the grounds that they could no longer ensure the Indians' safety in the light of the *contra* attacks being staged from across the border, and that they also wanted to prevent the *contra* using the Miskito community as a recruiting area. Shortly before the relocation they claimed to have uncovered a *contra* plot (known as 'Red Christmas') to provoke a Miskito uprising and subsequently to appropriate their territory. The destruction of Miskito property after the Indians had been removed was designed to prevent the occupation of the region by the *contra*. The problem the Miskitos posed for the Sandinistas was compounded by the fact that historically they had lived in virtual isolation from the majority of the Nicaraguan people – whom they called 'the Spanish' – and had treated them with suspicion and hostility. The Sandinistas later acknowledged their mishandling of the affair and in mid-1985 decided to allow the Miskitos to return to their original lands.

The bishops' claim that the Sandinistas violated human rights in the Miskito region is substantiated by the findings of some independent investigations. An Amnesty International report suggested that between July and October 1982 seventy-two Miskitos disappeared following arrest by the authorities, and Amnesty also expressed concern at the abrupt and peremptory manner in which the relocation was carried out and the hardship and suffering it caused.[2] It did, however, note that no cases of shooting or deliberate brutality during the transfer had been found, though subsequent cases of human rights violations, some against suspected *contra* supporters, were mentioned.

Criticism of the government's human rights record increased following the state of emergency, and the bishops protested against the arbitrary detention, interrogation and inhuman treatment of church-people, including priests. Sandinista officials confirmed that a policy of interrogation had been enforced, but that the priests involved were guilty of acting outside the law. Groups sympathetic to the Nicaraguan government have also expressed concern at the increasing militarization of the country in the face of *contra* attacks, and Amnesty International has drawn attention to the 'extraordinary *de facto* powers accorded the State Security Service under the state of emergency, and the consequent scope for abuse of these powers', and to cases where prisoners of conscience, among whom they included Fr Peña, have been detained or imprisoned.[3] Criticism of the treatment of detainees in some prisons was also made. Yet observers have also noted that the Sandinistas' human rights record compares favourably with that of some of its neighbours and with that of Somoza. Among the changes introduced by the revolution were the abolition of the death penalty and a more liberal penal system which included some use of 'open prisons'. These prisons, which have an emphasis on reform rather than retribution, have been instrumental in the rehabilitation of a number of ex-Somoza guardsmen. In some cases of human rights violation by the military, formal penalties have been imposed on those responsible, and in 1984 thirteen army officers received long prison sentences after convictions for murder and torture carried out in response to a *contra* attack.

The young

Conflict between the bishops and the government has also arisen over the issue of education, particularly that of children which traditionally has been the prerogative of the church. The bishops' concern is that the Sandinistas have used school curricula and educational projects as vehicles for spreading their own ideology and maintaining support for their régime. In October 1980 they referred in a pastoral letter to a 'siege of materialistic ideologies' confronting the church, and went on to assert 'the right of parents to educate

53

their children according to their Christian conviction', an apparent indication of a revival of interest in an area they formerly controlled. In their Easter 1984 letter they again spoke of a 'materialistic and atheistic educational system . . . undermining the consciences of our children and young people'.

Clearly the Sandinistas' educational policy has political intent, though Christians sympathetic to it deny it amounts to Marxist indoctrination. Fernando Cardenal, the priest who directed the Literacy Crusade, acknowledged that its aim was primarily to equip the people to participate in the political process, but defined the dominant ideology underpinning the educational system to be *sandinismo*, a belief in sovereignty, independence and national pride, and not Marxism-Leninism. The fact that a priest was entrusted with oversight of the crusade, and another leading Catholic figure, Carlos Tunnermann, appointed minister of education for the first five years of the revolution, could also be pointed to as evidence that government policy in this area was not rigidly Marxist. Religious schools have also continued to operate since the revolution and have received financial assistance from the government. Nevertheless, the state take-over of education, and the establishment of a single unified system for both public and private schools, has given rise to conflict between the bishops and the government.

Another area of controversy has been the introduction of patriotic military service, or conscription, which the church hierarchy has opposed on the grounds that it promotes Sandinista ideology particularly among the young. The bishops do not contest the right of the state to build a defensive military force, but they maintain that Nicaragua is a special case since the army does not principally serve the national interest but that of a single political party, the FSLN, and its ideology. Their opposition to compulsory military service, and open encouragement to Nicaraguans to become conscientious objectors, has brought reprisals from the government and was almost certainly behind the confiscation of the new church newspaper *Iglesia* in 1985.

What emerges from this discussion is that the differences between the Catholic hierarchy and the Sandinista government are essentially political rather than religious. The bishops are clearly justified in seeing the government as a threat, but the government's hostility appears to stem not from the fact that the bishops represent a church whose spiritual teaching offends their materialistic ideology, but from a suspicion that behind many of their actions and statements lies a deeper motivation which amounts to outright political opposition. The government's response to cases cited by the bishops as examples of persecution bears this out. It defended the suppression of the Pope's letters on grounds of their political sensitivity, and the expulsion of the foreign priests as a legitimate response to perceived anti-government activity. The exile of Bishop Vega was clearly a reaction to his apparent sympathy with United States' policies toward Nicaragua – both he and Mgr Carballo were accused of treason by President Daniel Ortega – and the censorship imposed on Obando's sermons and Radio Católica can also be interpreted as measures designed to limit access to the mass media by the political opposition. It is probably also no coincidence that Frs Carballo and Peña, victims of what appeared to be frame-ups by the Sandinistas, were both outspoken critics of the government and close associates of Cardinal Obando y Bravo. Finally, the bishops' criticisms of conscription at a time of increased activity by the counter-revolutionary forces would also have been seen by the Sandinistas as subversive.

In the period since the revolution church and state have effectively become caught in a perpetual spiral of suspicion. The punitive measures the government has taken against the church, whatever their motive, have served to increase its fears that the FSLN is fundamentally anti-clerical and has a long-term aim to eliminate the church; and the Sandinistas for their part have become increasingly concerned about the church hierarchy's role as a focus for the political opposition, and the possibility that it may be prepared to act as a fifth column in the interests of outside agencies bent on destabilizing the régime. As the external threats to the government have increased, and created greater tension inside the country, so suspicion has deepened on both sides. The Sandinistas' fears about the church will not have been lessened by their awareness that the United States appears in favour of using religious institutions to counteract popular revolutions. As far back as 1968 the Rockefeller Report spoke of the need for such a course, and the more recent Santa Fe Report, which appears to be underpinning many of the Reagan administration's foreign policy decisions, maintains that:

The foreign policy of the US must begin to confront and not simply to react to the Theology of Liberation as it is utilized in Latin America . . . Unfortunately, Marxist forces have utilized the Church as a political weapon against private property and the capitalist system of production by infiltrating the religious community with ideas which are less Christian than Communist.[4]

Perhaps only time will tell whether the bishops have been justified in their perception that the Sandinista government poses an ultimate threat to the church. Officially the FSLN has displayed a consistent respect for religious belief, as their manifestos of 1969 and 1984, and the 1980 communiqué on religion, testify. As an official statement of policy this latter document differed significantly from others which have been issued by revolutionary movements in power. It went further than giving a guarantee that the freedom to profess religious belief would be upheld, and acknowledged that a Christian faith can inspire and motivate revolutionary commitment. It recognized and commended the participation by Christians in the revolutionary process, and mentioned by name Gaspar García and others, including Delegates of the Word, who were 'exemplary in their willingness to die and shed their blood to make the seed of liberation grow'. It also paid tribute to Obando y Bravo and the other bishops for courageously denouncing Somoza and suffering harassment as a consequence. 'Our experience has shown,' the document continued, 'that it is possible to be a believer and a committed revolutionary at the same time and that there is no irreconcilable contradiction between the two.'

Evidence that this is a consensus view among the FSLN may be drawn from César Jerez' analysis of attitudes to religion among Front members.[5] Jerez identifies a wide range of positions within the Front, but suggests that only a small and uninfluential group subscribes to a dogmatic Marxist-Leninist interpretation of religion, in contrast to the majority who have either some form of religious belief (albeit in many cases latent) or a degree of sympathy with the Catholic faith. According to critics of the FSLN, however, its conciliatory attitude towards religion should not be taken at face value. Humberto Belli has argued that the FSLN has always been a Marxist-Leninist organization which, for strategic reasons, adopted in 1978 'a more cautious ideological profile' to attract the support of non-Marxist sectors of society including the church. On coming to power it made a concerted effort, conscious of the depth of religious feeling in the country, to avoid exposing its commitment to an atheistic ideology and its intentions to undermine the church. For Belli the FSLN's openness to religion was a façade necessitated by the fact that in a country with a strong religious culture it is politically suicidal to adopt an atheistic or anti-religious platform. Bismark Carballo has also spoken of the FSLN's Marxism and materialism not becoming apparent until after the revolution. Another critic of the Sandinista régime, Miguel Bolaños Hunter, has maintained that the FSLN made a point of recruiting priests sympathetic to liberation theology into its ranks in order to compromise them and guarantee their future loyalty because it feared that in time their theology could become a threat to it. Bolaños, a former Sandinista state security agent, also alleged that the FSLN wanted to use liberation theology to divide the church, and had plans to encourage young Sandinistas to train to become evangelical pastors or Catholic priests to ensure the future commitment of the churches to the revolution.[6] The claim that the Sandinistas planned to divide and conquer the church has also been made by Belli and by members of the church hierarchy, including Obando y Bravo and Bismark Carballo, who have all referred to documents published secretly by the FSLN which outline this intent.

Priests within the Sandinista organization offer a different interpretation. For Ernesto and Fernando Cardenal the government's policy of appointing priests and Catholic lay-people to important government posts – covering foreign affairs, economic planning, literacy, education, ideology and 'the most precious thing it has: its youth . . . its future' – indicates the confidence it has in members of the church. Such a policy, it has also been argued, does not appear consistent with any long-term plans to eliminate the Christian faith. But to others such arguments are worthless, since the ideology of the priests in the government appears essentially no different from that of any non-Christian Sandinista: their identification with Marxism has overwhelmed their Christian identity.

Two things may be said in conclusion. First, if the bishops' request for the priests in the government to resign is heeded, then their fears that the administration will ultimately prove to be atheistic would seem more likely to be realized – unless, that is, they share the view that the priests are already so compromised that they provide no distinctive Christian witness in the process anyway. Secondly, what appears to be of primary importance to the FSLN, on the evidence of their speeches and documents, is not so much an individual's religious beliefs as her or his political commitment. Religious faith is acknowledged or rejected primarily according to the political stance it inspires, and where it is not used for counter-revolutionary purposes the practice of Christianity is given free rein. As their official statement on religion clearly spelt out, 'Naturally, Sandinistas are good friends of Christian revolutionaries but not of the counter-revolutionaries, even though they call themselves Christian.' How far the Sandinistas have carried this through in practice may be judged by the testimonies of many priests sympathetic to the Front which, in contrast to those of most official church spokespeople, point to an absence of religious persecution in the country (and more to the pressures placed upon them by their own church leadership). In short, belief or non-belief, providing it does not hinder a commitment to the revolution, appears to be of small consequence. 'It shouldn't concern me if you believe there is something after death, nor should it interest you if I think that after death I'm going to rot here,' FSLN commander Oscar Turcios once told Fernando Cardenal. 'What should concern us is that we can both work together to build a new Nicaragua.'[7]

5 · Political Priests and a Polish Pope

The controversy surrounding the priests in the Sandinista government has been the longest and perhaps most divisive in post-
revolutionary Nicaragua, symbolizing the tensions the revolution has
generated among Christians in the country and within the Catholic
church as a whole. Here we shall consider the effect it has had on the
Nicaraguan church, and the influence of the Vatican hierarchy both
on this particular issue and on church-state relations in Nicaragua in
general.

The four priests at the centre of the dispute are Miguel D'Escoto
and Ernesto Cardenal, who became, respectively, Foreign Minister
and Minister of Culture when the revolutionary government was
installed; Fernando Cardenal, who was appointed Minister of
Education on 13 July 1984, having previously served as national co-
ordinator of the Literacy Crusade and vice-coordinator of the
Sandinista Youth Movement; and Edgar Parrales, Minister of Social
Welfare from 1980 until 1982, when he became ambassador to the
Organization of American States. Parrales and Ernesto Cardenal, as
diocesan priests, are responsible to their bishops, whereas D'Escoto
and Fernando Cardenal, as members respectively of the Maryknoll
Fathers and the Society of Jesus, answer to the superiors of those
orders. Other priests who held less prominent posts within the
government, for example the Nicaraguan Clergy Association
(ACLEN) delegate to the Council of State, Alvaro Argüello, have
also been implicated in the affair.

As the discussion in previous chapters has suggested, the priests
view their commitment to the revolution as entirely consistent with
their Christian faith and priestly calling. For them it is a process

making effective Medellín's preferential option for the poor, and the area of 'politics' is just one to which Christians are called to help consolidate that process. As Fernando Cardenal has summarized it,

> Our service of God in the priesthood has led us to the ministry of charity and love, which in Nicaragua has been translated into a ministry in support of the forward march of the people, the ministry of accompanying our people from within, by participating in a transformation of structures, so that the poor may have justice.[1]

Cardenal in fact sees his role in the revolutionary government as *more* consistent with a priestly calling than his previous career as a professor of philosophy which, though it also had no explicit relationship with the priesthood, attracted no opposition from the church. He argues that it would be harder to find a more secular occupation for a priest than expounding Leibnitz and Kant, whereas his work in the Literary Crusade fulfilled a gospel command to teach the uneducated. It was also consistent with Ignatius Loyola's directive to the Jesuits to set aside time to give instruction.

All four priests have individually and collectively stated their belief that they see no contradiction between their priestly and political duties. In a Confession of Faith signed on 8 June 1981 they affirmed:

> We have sought to serve our compatriots in the offices in which we have been placed by them. And we shall continue to do so . . . For our offices have given us: . . . the power to exercise our priest-hood, not to separate ourselves from our vocation . . .[2]

A year earlier they wrote, 'Our loyalty to the church and our loyalty to the poor cannot be in contradiction.'[3]

The Nicaraguan bishops, however, do not view involvement in a revolutionary government as consonant with a priestly calling. Although in the formative months of the revolution they were prepared to recognize the priests' activities as an exception, since May 1980 they have consistently called for all four to resign and be replaced by lay-people. The bishops' argument was that, although the church allowed political participation by priests in extraordinary circumstances or emergencies, such circumstances ceased to exist in Nicaragua in May 1980. To some extent this was a subjective view, and others in the church argued that whilst Nicaragua remained under threat from counter-revolutionary forces a state of emergency continued to exist, and therefore that the special talents which the priests could offer the country, through their participation in the government, ought not to be suppressed. They also wanted the church's solidarity with the poor, of which the priests' commitment to the revolution was a sign, to be maintained. In November 1983, however, the canon law permitting exceptional political activity by priests was repealed and a more blanket prohibition introduced, which made it easier for the bishops to argue, from that point on, that the priests were in direct contravention of church law.

The bishops have given other reasons for their opposition to the priests' position. First they expressed concern that the priests' identification with the government would cause division among their flock, and they reaffirmed the opinion of Puebla that a priest's duty is to symbolize unity in the church. Secondly they feared that the priests' position would lead to the church losing its identity. Thirdly they considered that the priests were not pursuing a specifically priestly ministry and, with a shortage of priests in the country, were needed in their parishes. Fourthly they maintained that the priests had allowed themselves to be instrumentalized by the Sandinistas and used as 'naive tools' for political ends. The bishops referred to the FSLN buying the services of the priests through patronage and flattery, and drew a comparison between their position and that of clerics in the past who gave their support to feudal powers. It is also clear from their statements that another central issue in the debate was authority. In their ultimatum of June 1981 they stipulated that if the priests did not resign as soon as possible,

> we would have to consider them to be in a position of open rebellion and formal disobedience to legitimate ecclesiastical authority, and thus subject to penalties provided by the laws of the church.

In a communiqué issued a month later they spoke of their 'temporary toleration' of the situation, and reiterated with 'absolute insistence' their directive that the priests return to their priestly ministry as soon as possible.

It is difficult to say to what extent the priests' position amounts to disobedience to the church. The bishops' original call to them to resign, in May 1980, was a request rather than a threat and, following discussions between the government and the Vatican, they were allowed to remain in post. When the bishops did issue an ultimatum, in June the following year, further visits to Rome by representatives of the government and the bishops again resulted in compromise, with all four being allowed to continue in the government provided that they abstained from all priestly functions including celebrating mass and administering the sacraments. In addition, the new code of canon law, although forbidding priests to assume public office or exercise civil power (Canon 285), contained no provision for that particular canon to be applied retroactively. This suggests that it could only have been applied to Fernando Cardenal, since the other three had already taken their government posts before it became operative on 27 November 1983. Nevertheless, in the view of the Vatican and the bishops the new code undermined the legal basis of the 1981 compromise, and by 1985 formal penalties had been imposed on all four priests. In December 1984 Fernando Cardenal was expelled from the Society of Jesus, and on 19 January 1985 he, his brother Ernesto, Parrales and D'Escoto were all suspended from the priesthood. Parrales later applied for full laicization. Despite Fernando's experience, D'Escoto's position within his order appears to be secure since his superior general has some sympathy with the Nicaraguan government. To some extent the suspensions imposed on the four must be seen as symbolic, since priesthood is recognized within the church as being for life, and none of the four had been allowed to perform priestly duties since 1981.

Not surprisingly the bishops' response has also been interpreted as further evidence of their opposition to the government. Some observers have argued that they wanted the priests to leave the government because they feared it would become totalitarian and anti-Christian, and they wanted to avoid appearing to identify the church with it. Fernando Cardenal alleged that political rather than pastoral concerns were behind the original opposition in the church to his involvement in the government. He suggested in an open letter of December 1984 that calls for him to leave the revolution, at a time when it was under attack from counter-revolutionary forces, showed that some Nicaraguan bishops had 'a political agenda that today, as yesterday, openly contradicts the interests of the majority of the poor people'. In this letter, written shortly before his suspension from the priesthood, he went on to assert that, the rigid application of Canon 285.3 cannot help but appear in Nicaragua as a pretext to use us in an attempt to undermine the Revolution, uniting this action to a series of all kinds of aggression which the U.S. Government and its allies are directing against our little country.

A lack of pastoral concern by the bishops was evident, he claimed, from the way his requests for an audience with them to discuss his position met with no reply. Cardenal also dismissed the argument that the country has too few priests in parish work, alleging that the bishops had not shown concern about other priests with no parish commitments such as those who are teachers. Observers have also noted that during the Somoza years there were never any calls from the bishops for National Guard chaplains who were priests to resign.

The issue of the priests in the Sandinista government has been more than a conflict between two factions within the Nicaraguan church, and the Catholic hierarchy in Rome has also been involved throughout. A number of official visits were made by government and church representatives to the Vatican in 1980 and 1981 to discuss the matter, and Pope John Paul II made references to it in his letter to the bishops of 29 June 1982 and in his address in Managua on 4 March 1983. The Vatican's attitude to the issue, and to Nicaraguan church-state relations in general, is important for an overall understanding of the situation.

It is clear from the Pope's letter and address that he sees the presence of priests in the Sandinista government as detrimental to the unity of the church, and perhaps a further manifestation of the threat to the church which is posed by the 'popular church' and its theology of liberation. A re-emphasis of the importance of unity has therefore been the central theme of the Pope's messages to the Nicaraguan church, though it is important to understand what has motivated this concern. On the one hand it has arisen from a belief that the church must be a symbol or sacrament of unity, both in the country and among all people, but alongside this appears also to be a fear that a breakdown of unity in the church will lead to a breakdown of papal and episcopal authority. Thus the Pope has been concerned to stress, in his calls for unity in the church, that this unity must always be built around its 'lawful pastors', specifically the bishops and himself as Pope. To John Paul the principal crime of the 'popular church' is that it exists alongside or even in opposition to the church headed by the bishops, and the error of the priests in government is that they have not submitted to 'the magisterium of the church, represented by the pope and bishops', and have broken the unity of the church by 'acting outside of or against the will of the bishops "whom the Holy Spirit has set to guide the church of God" (Acts 20.28)'.[4]

It is clear that radically different ecclesiological models have shaped the attitudes of the Pope and the priests in government. For John Paul the most appropriate role for the church to play in society appears to be one based on a version of the old Christendom model where church and state, though independent of each other, collaborate and provide mutual legitimation. Yet although this model may have guided the church in Poland, with whatever lack of success, it has been explicitly rejected by the priests in the Nicaraguan government, who in no sense see their relationship with the civil authorities in those terms. They describe their involvement in a revolutionary government as 'serving the people' and, as such, symbolic of the church's renunciation of its past alliances with ruling élites. To the Pope, however, their complete identification with a civil government compromises the church and sacrifices its independent authority.

The Pope has taken a strong line on the question of the priests in government, offering little by way of reasoned argument for his position but making their resignation a matter of straightforward obedience to papal *fiat*. Whilst this attitude has aroused some criticism, not least from those it has most directly affected, it should perhaps be understood within the context of the profound changes taking place in other parts of the Latin American church which are perceived to be undermining Rome's authority. The emergence of liberation theology, for example, has increasingly worried the Vatican,[5] not only because it makes political commitment *a priori* and uses Marxist categories of social analysis and the language of class struggle, but because it also leads very often to a rejection of the whole hierarchical structure of the church. It is not likely, for example, that a church committed to political liberation will want to organize itself according to the pattern of traditional Catholic hierarchies. Thus the tendency for some Christians in Latin America to promote a church *of* rather than just *for* the poor, as evidenced by the growing number of CEBs, is responsible at least in part for the Pope's increasing emphasis on the need for unity in the church to be maintained around the hierarchy. Aware that by the end of the century half the world's Catholics will be in Latin America, the Vatican has not failed to realize the implications of a loss of its authority over the church there now. The struggle to contain liberation theology, the base communities and the church of the poor is part of the battle for the whole of Latin America, and it is in this wider context that the Pope's concern over the priests in the Nicaraguan government should perhaps be viewed.

It is not unlikely that the Pope's attitude to the priests in government has also been influenced by a distaste for Marxism born of a lifetime's experience of one form of it as a priest and bishop in Poland. His unwillingness to see the church become involved with a Marxist-led administration may explain his reluctance to allow the Sandinista priests to keep their ministerial posts, when a dispensation of this sort appears to have been made for a Jesuit priest holding a government position in Colombia.[6] Ernesto Cardenal has suggested that the problem in Nicaragua is that the priests in the government there are revolutionaries, and for the Pope Christianity and revolution do not go together.

The Pope's position is not one of opposition to political liberation or a preferential option for the poor as such, and in his visits to Latin America he has repeatedly touched on social and economic issues and affirmed the church's commitment to the cause of justice and its solidarity with the needy and suffering. What he does oppose, and has consistently condemned, is the use of violence or non-Christian ideologies as a means of achieving a new social order. 'You rightly feel – and should always feel – the longing for a more just society,' he told a gathering of Peruvian Christians during a visit in February 1985, 'but do not follow those who say that social injustice can only disappear through hatred between classes or the resort to violence and other anti-Christian methods.'[7] The social doctrine of the church, he told Colombians during a speech in July 1986 in which he called for higher wages, agrarian reform and a sharing of wealth, 'excludes . . . the organized struggle of classes which leads to new forms of slavery'.[8] For the Pope, the church and the bishops have a specifically religious role in society 'which is not identical with nor a substitute for the politicians, economists, sociologists, intellectuals or labour leaders'. This role is to foster a genuine and full humanism, and to assert otherwise means 'distracting the church from its primary mission and identifying it with other interests on the basis of a dangerous and destructive reductionism'.[9]

Although the Pope described his visit to Nicaragua on 4 March 1983 as primarily religious, the messages he delivered on that occasion were perceived by many to have anti-régime overtones. The tone of his visit was set right at the start when, during a welcoming ceremony at Managua's Sandino airport, he publicly rebuked Ernesto Cardenal as the priest knelt to kiss the papal ring. At Leon, to a largely *campesino* audience, he expressed his concern at the shift towards a secular schooling policy in Nicaragua, and defended the right of all to receive a Christian education. He also made a veiled attack on liberation theology, dismissing the notion that 'alien ideologies' can add anything to the church's teaching on love and human dignity. He then moved on to celebrate mass in the capital, an event which was to generate even greater political tension.

At least three factors contributed to this. First the Pope's call for unity, the central theme of his message, was interpreted by some as undermining the option for the poor which they believed the revolution was attempting to make concrete. Secondly his plea for this unity to be built around the bishops appeared, in view of their known antipathy to the process, to be a call to join them in opposing the revolution. An FSLN communiqué, issued within a few days of the Pope's visit, noted the political significance of this part of the Pope's speech. And thirdly, although he commended the Nicaraguan people for their heroism in the face of the natural disasters they had faced, he made no specific reference to their struggle to remove Somoza, their attempts to build a new society, or their resistance to the *contras*, achievements which many in the crowd would also have wanted to describe as heroic. His omission of any reference to the *contra* attacks caused particular surprise, especially since the funeral of seventeen young people killed in one such attack had been held the previous day, in the plaza where he was speaking.

Some observers have also suggested that, whatever may have been the Pope's personal view, the mass itself was organized to make a political point even through the selection of readings and prayers. Ernesto Cardenal has noted that no prayer was offered for those who govern, though, he maintains, it is in the text of every mass and is used by the Pope in every country he visits no matter how good or bad the government. Cardenal has also criticized the choice of a reading on the Tower of Babel which, he says, had no relevance to the situation in Nicaragua but implied that the government was proud and arrogant and wanted to substitute itself for God. 'In the text, those who built the Tower of Babel were lifting themselves as high as God, and then God destroyed everyone. *That* was the message.'[10] Observers also found significant the choice of another reading, the story of the Good Shepherd. Yet although the tone of the whole service and the content of the Pope's address may explain to some extent the hostile reaction of some in the crowd, the whole occasion appears to have been a further example of the way in which a specifically religious event could assume, in Nicaragua's tense post-revolutionary climate, enormous political significance.

Accusations have been made, for example, that the government planned in advance to turn the event into a political demonstration by encouraging agitators to shout pro-Sandinista slogans and by having technicians ensure those slogans were heard above the Pope's message. The government was also accused of halting traffic to prevent many Catholics reaching the plaza, and the Pope on several occasions made reference to those who had been debarred from attending the mass. Counter-claims, however, suggest that far from restricting access to the mass, the government allocated two months' supply of petrol to encourage people to attend, and around 700,000, a quarter of the entire population, responded. The Sandinistas, it is claimed, would have been committing political suicide by trying to use the occasion to insult the Pope, since a successful visit would have been much more in their interest and would have helped to strengthen their claims of a sympathetic stance towards religion. The restlessness in the crowd has been explained by the Pope's increasingly cold and at times authoritarian tone – perhaps in part due to a failure to appreciate the culture and new self-assertiveness of the people since the revolution – and his refusal to console those who had been bereaved by *contra* attacks. Clearly much confusion surrounds the event, but given the fact that the Nicaraguan church was deeply divided over its attitude to the revolution and the government there was no way that, by visiting the country as head of that church, the Pope could avoid becoming involved himself in the political drama.

Among possible explanations for the Pope's general stance towards Nicaragua, perhaps the most plausible is that he or those who advise him interpret the situation in rather black-and-white Eastern European terms. One of the briefing documents for the 1983 Central American tour advised the Nicaraguan church and the Vatican that a policy of accommodation with the Sandinistas could not succeed since theirs was a Marxist-Leninist government and therefore an enemy of the church irremediably committed to its destruction. Vice-President Ramírez's perception was that the Pope failed to understand the situation in Nicaragua because he tried to interpret it against the background of his experience as a Pole:

> He came here with a preconceived notion. He thought that here was a totalitarian régime that oppressed the Catholic people and that these Catholics would take advantage of his presence to start a rebellion. He thought this was the opportunity they were waiting for to 'liberate themselves' from religious persecution. Basically, he got off the plane as an ideological conquistador.[11]

Observers have noted that a number of people unsympathetic to the Sandinista régime, including leading US politicians, officials of CELAM, and Archbishop Obando, travelled to Costa Rica to see the Pope before he entered Nicaragua, although it is believed that in the months preceding the Central American trip he also had before him a brief prepared by priests more committed to the Sandinista line. Another influential figure behind the planning for the Pope's 1983 visit is thought to have been Humberto Belli, a Nicaraguan who in 1982 was appointed to the Vatican as an advisor at the Secretariat for Non-Believers. Belli has written of the church in his country facing a choice between taking a Polish option, where it is not afraid to confront the government, and a Czech option where it becomes subservient to the régime. Belli favours the first, and has referred to Cardinal Obando as the Wyszyński of 'the Poland of Central America'.[12]

If the Vatican did apply a Polish model of church-state relations in Nicaragua it would go a long way towards explaining the tension that underlay the Pope's visit. In many important respects the government and church in Nicaragua did not resemble their Polish counterparts, and whereas in his native country the Pope could tap into a mood of general estrangement from the government shared by a united church, in Nicaragua it was not the same. The deep divisions among both church and people which had arisen in the wake of the revolution created a very different atmosphere, and a failure to recognize this projected the Pope into a potentially explosive situation which wittingly or otherwise his mass at Managua ignited.

The Pope's stance on Nicaragua does not appear to have changed markedly since his 1983 visit. The elevation of Archbishop Obando to cardinal in 1985, the first ever case in the Central American church, was widely interpreted as a move to increase his authority in the church and the country. The suspension three months earlier of the four priests in the government, though consistent with church teaching that priests must avoid political activity, also appeared to signal the Pope's continued concern over their identification with a government ideologically opposed to the church. Shortly after their suspension the head of the Maryknoll Order claimed on his return from a visit to Rome that the Vatican authorities considered the Sandinista administration 'an out-and-out Marxist government, with no redeeming values'.[13] The Nicaraguan government's hostility to the church was also a theme in the Pope's letter of December 1985 in which he sympathized with the 'painful situation' in which the bishops found themselves, and noted that many obstacles were placed in the way of the Nicaraguan church, including intimidation and the ill-treatment and expulsion of priests and laity. Unity around the bishops was once again the best defence for a community 'forced to live out its faith under these conditions'. 'With your hearts and faces turned towards your pastors, I exhort you to follow their words and their guidance,' he wrote. How far such calls will be heeded, though, may depend less on how often they are made and more on how credible the bishops' opposition to the government appears in the light of future developments. But however the revolution develops, the enormous influence the Catholic church exerts in Nicaragua suggests the Vatican's concern with events in that country is hardly set to diminish.

6 · A Better Mañana?

For two decades or more after the Second World War the church in Latin America talked liberation – not just a spiritual release from the debilitating effects of moral guilt to be gained by individual reconciliation with God, but social, political and economic emancipation to be won by collective action, structural change and if necessary violent revolution. Over many years it debated principles, developed theologies, issued statements and forged strategic alliances with revolutionary movements. Yet the hoped-for liberation remained only a vision until, in Nicaragua, that highly combustible combination of economic inequality and a repressive and disliked dictatorship was finally lit by a strong and highly popular revolutionary movement, and the church was faced with the prospect of participating in a project which could create the conditions for building the just society for which it had looked. It responded to the challenge, and for the first time in modern history a revolutionary transfer of power was accomplished with the blessing of the institutional Catholic church and the active support of many of its members. Che Guevara had once said that 'when Christians will dare to give a total revolutionary testimony the Latin American revolution will be invincible',[1] and thus far he had been proved right. But what would be the consequences of this excursion into the realm of practical revolutionary commitment?

For the Nicaraguan church the experience of living in a revolutionary situation partly of its own creation has involved enduring a deep internal rift and the possibility of eventual schism. Divided fundamentally over its attitude to the Sandinistas and the way they have followed through the revolution, the church has found itself both inside and outside the government, committed to furthering the revolution and to halting its progress. At the root of this disunity, as we have noted, lie profoundly different conceptions of the role the church should play in the new post-revolutionary situation. For some Christians the changed political and social order offers the church new opportunities for evangelization, defined as praxis in the interests of the poor, and for ecclesial reform to reflect this new emphasis. To others the revolution has given up its original ideals and become hardened inside the totalitarian and anti-clerical mould into which all revolutions eventually drop, and has left the church no alternative but to try to reverse the process in the interests of its own survival. For them, the Christians still committed to the process have either compromised their faith virtually out of existence, or been deceived into supporting a régime bent ultimately on the destruction of the church. The anti-Sandinista grouping, which includes most of the bishops, appears committed to more traditional models of the church, and to the restoration of a politico-economic system, perhaps a form of *somocismo* without Somoza, to which such models are better suited. We have also seen that class explanations for these intra-church divisions may be appropriate, and are often recognized by those sympathetic to the revolutionary process, although amongst a hierarchy which still appears to see the church as a unity above class conflict they have to be rejected in favour of ecclesiological ones. Thus there is, within a divided church, further disagreement over the causes of its divisions, which indicates the depth of the cleft that has opened up among Nicaraguan Catholics since the revolution.

What has made this polarization appear even more acute has been the tendency for the church to become a focus for opposing factions within Nicaragua as a whole. Whether by default or design Cardinal Obando has emerged as an important, if not the leading opposition figure to the government, and many of his pastoral visits around the country have assumed additional significance as anti-government rallies. On the pro-government side Christians and others who support the Sandinistas have grouped around the priests in the government, with Miguel D'Escoto emerging as a particularly prominent figure. In July 1985 D'Escoto began a month-long fast to highlight what he called the US government's 'state terrorism' against Nicaragua and the country's 'right to life and self-determination', and during Lent the following year led a 'way of the cross' for peace from Jalapa on the northern frontier to Managua. Both activities drew support from Christians and others sympathetic to the government. The Lenten *via crucis* also attracted strong criticism from the Vatican newspaper *L'Osservatore Romano*, which accused D'Escoto of using a devotional exercise for political ends. The paper asked whether it was too late to hope for a 'genuine evangelical gesture' from D'Escoto, 'a moment of inner clarity that would remind him that before Christ, before the church, before the Nicaraguan people and above all before himself he is first of all a priest'.[2] In a sense this episode neatly crystallizes the gap in understanding that has emerged within the Catholic church, since for D'Escoto his Lenten march was just such a gesture, a symbol of his hopes for peace and justice in Nicaragua and of the 'gospel insurrection' which he wanted his fast in 1985 to incite to hasten the arrival of these kingdom values in society.

The relative strengths of the opposing factions within the Nicaraguan church is hard to assess, though observers have suggested that up to a quarter of priests and religious have remained behind the revolution, with the rest taking either an independent or pro-hierarchy line. Not surprisingly, accurate figures are hard to come by, and all estimates are liable to vary depending on the political bias of the source. For example, the number of people who turned out to welcome Archbishop Obando when he returned from Rome following his investiture as a cardinal varies from 30,000 to 500,000 depending on who is providing the figures. Some idea of D'Escoto's support may be inferred from the fact that roughly one third of the country's priests concelebrated or attended the mass which marked the end of his 'way of the cross' in 1986. But perhaps the largest group is the mass of ordinary Catholics who are both confused and uneasy about the conflict between the bishops and the Sandinistas, and hopeful that dialogue can still be maintained as a way of restoring peace and reconciliation within the church.

In the long term these estimates may be of little value, since the future direction of the Nicaraguan church is likely to depend less on the extent to which conservative and radical clergy are able to rally support for their respective positions than on the direction taken by the revolution itself. If it is able to fulfil popular expectations of it then a position of support may come to be widely seen as a valid

Christian option: if, however, it is increasingly perceived to be only marginally better than the system which it replaced, or if it moves or is pushed in the direction of totalitarianism and anti-clericalism, then the church could become an important focus of popular opposition.

Whether or not the revolution will survive, and if so in what form, will depend on a number of internal and especially external factors. Despite their solid victory in the 1984 elections, support for the Sandinistas has waned since the revolution, and the rise in living standards which the revolution promised has not yet materialized. World recession, cuts in foreign aid, unfavourable trade terms, a debt crisis and some internal inefficiencies have all combined to weaken the economy and undermine support for the government. Cuts in government expenditure have been made affecting key areas like education and health. But perhaps the biggest single threat to the stability of Nicaragua and its revolution is that posed by the United States government, whose campaign against the country, through the use of economic sanctions, military force and *contra* groups, has dealt a major blow to its economy and forced the Sandinistas to divert much of their energy and resources away from internal development and towards defence. The Sandinistas claimed that US hostility was also behind their decision to tighten internal security and impose a state of emergency, measures which undermined still further their support in the country. To the Reagan administration Nicaragua has all the hallmarks of a totalitarian Marxist state and, although no military threat in itself, has the potential to become a new Soviet base just a few hundred miles from the US border. Its revolution was also of course a threat to US strategic and economic interests in Central America. To what extent US hostility has been used by the Sandinistas as an excuse for all the country's ills is a point of debate, but there is clearly some credibility to their claim that all the apparent failures of the revolution must be seen within the context of the war being waged against the country.[3]

The use of the *contras* has to some extent been effective in destabilizing the country, in that many thousands of Nicaraguans have died in the fighting, and extensive damage has been caused to land, property and crops. However, the reports which have emerged of their terror and brutality, against the civilian population as well as the Sandinista militia, have cost the Reagan government much

73

support, and some of the most outspoken criticism has come from the churches in the United States itself. In 1983 the Catholic bishops called for an end to their government's hostile position towards Nicaragua, and in 1986 urged Congress to reject President Reagan's request for a $100 million aid package to the *contras*[4]. The Bishop of Detroit was also among religious leaders who had earlier set up a fund to raise money for the Nicaraguan government to match that given by their own to the *contras*. Small groups of US Christians under the banner of 'Witness for Peace' have set up camps along the Honduran border as a means of non-violent protest against their government's aggression towards Nicaragua, and thousands more back home have formally pledged their resistance to the policy. Many Christians are clearly questioning President Reagan's right to wage war against a smaller country not itself acting aggressively towards the United States, and are also concerned that his apparent commitment to an East-West analysis of the situation has hidden the possibility that it might also be a North- South issue, and that the Sandinista revolution may offer to people in the Third World a model of escape from the dehumanizing poverty and powerlessness which enslaves so many.

Other factors may also have a bearing on Nicaragua's future. One is the Contadora initiative, begun in 1983 by Colombia, Mexico, Panama and Venezuela, which has tried, so far unsuccessfully, to solve the crisis in Central America by means of negotiation and dialogue. Another is the role of the Vatican which has generally been unsympathetic to the Sandinista régime. Whether the perpetuation of the revolution will eventually encourage Rome to adopt a more accommodating policy towards it remains to be seen, although in July 1986 Vice-President Ramírez reported, on his return from a visit to the Pope, that he had had a constructive and cordial meeting which had opened up prospects for a long-term understanding between the Sandinistas and the Catholic church. Attempts to settle the differences between the church and the government were also made at a meeting the following month between President Ortega and the new Papal Nuncio to Nicaragua, Archbishop Paolo Giglio, and at the end of September, possibly at the instigation of Giglio, Ortega and Cardinal Obando met to discuss the issues dividing them. The two leaders agreed to hold a series of talks aimed at working out, as Ortega put it, 'an accord between the govenment and the church to normalize and stabilize relations',[5] with issues on the agenda to include the position of Bishop Vega and Mgr Carballo and the continued closure of Radio Católica. By late 1986 it was being reported that the talks had produced an agreement that church and state would 'respect each other's autonomy', and that the government might be prepared to allow the church radio station to re-open with the proviso that it would not be used for anti-government purposes.[6] In what was seen as another significant development President Ortega met Mother Teresa in Nicaragua in November and announced that the government had agreed, after its initial refusal, to allow her Missionaries of Charity to work in the country. Viewed against the background of the Vatican's 1986 statement on liberation theology, which was considerably more positive in tone than the earlier Instruction issued in 1984, these factors appear to suggest that the prospects for constructive dialogue and peaceful co-existence between Rome, the Nicaraguan church and the Sandinista government were better at the beginning of 1987 than they had been for some time.

A third factor will be the fate of the revolutionary movements in states like El Salvador and Guatemala, since a successful revolution in one or more of these neighbouring countries might well enhance the long-term prospects of the Sandinista régime in Nicaragua. By the same token the failure of such movements could increase further Nicaragua's isolation in the region, and raise even more starkly the spectre of a once vibrant and popular revolution becoming hardened and entrenched, with internal militarization and repression the necessary price to pay for survival. What is certain, however, is that not only will the church in Nicaragua be affected by developments both internal and external, it will also be itself a determining factor in the country's future.

Further reading

Readers should note that the vast majority of recent literature on Nicaragua available in the UK has been written from a position of broad support for the revolution and the Sandinistas. This is not to say that all of it is uncritical, but, outside occasional articles in journals and magazines, very little appears to have been produced by writers fundamentally opposed to the Nicaraguan government or supportive of the US interpretation of the situation in the country. That having been said, the following books and articles may be of interest to those wishing to explore further some of the topics raised in this book.

The most comprehensive study of the role of the church in the Nicaraguan revolution is Philip Berryman, *The Religious Roots of Rebellion*, Orbis Books and SCM Press 1984. Berryman covers events down to mid-1982 (with a short postscript added in 1983), and also reflects on some of the issues raised by Christian involvement in revolutionary activity. The experience of the church in El Salvador and Guatemala is also covered. For a shorter introduction see Michael Dodson and T. S. Montgomery, 'The Churches in the Nicaraguan Revolution', *Nicaragua in Revolution*, ed. Thomas Walker, Praeger 1982, and the more analytical surveys by César Jerez, *The Church and the Nicaraguan Revolution*, CIIR 1984, and Luis Serra, 'Ideology, Religion and the Class Struggle in the Nicaraguan Revolution', *Nicaragua: A Revolution under Siege*, ed. Richard Harris and Carlos M. Vilas, Zed Books 1985. For a more critical account see Humberto Belli, 'The Church in Nicaragua: Under Attack From Within and Without', *Religion in Communist Lands*, Vol. 12, No. 1, Spring 1984. For a discussion of the position of the non-Catholic churches in Nicaragua see David Haslam, *Faith in Struggle: The Protestant Churches in Nicaragua and Their Response to the Revolution*, Epworth Press 1987. Trevor Beeson and Jenny Pearce, *A Vision of Hope: the Churches and Change in Latin America*, Collins, Fount Paperbacks 1984, and Penny Lernoux, *Cry of the People*, Penguin Books 1982, provide more general perspectives on the church in Latin America as does Enrique Dussel's classic study *A History of the Church in Latin America*, Eerdmans 1981. Sergio Torres and John Eagleson (eds.), *The Challenge of Basic Christian Communities*, Orbis Books 1981, contains a number of articles dealing with Nicaragua.

For primary material see Teófilo Cabestrero, *Ministers of God, Ministers of the People*, Orbis Books and Zed Press 1983, which contains wide-ranging interviews with Ernesto Cardenal, Fernando Cardenal and Miguel D'Escoto. Shorter interviews with the Cardenal brothers and with Edgar Parrales, Bismark Carballo and other church-people appear in Philip Zwerling & Connie Martin (eds.), *Nicaragua – A New Kind of Revolution*, Lawrence Hill 1985. The Solentiname discussions have been published in four volumes – Ernesto Cardenal, *The Gospel in Solentiname*, Orbis Books 1976–82 – but a good sampler is Philip and Sally Scharper (eds.), *The Gospel in Art by the Peasants of Solentiname*, Orbis Books and Gill & Macmillan 1984, which contains over thirty beautiful full-colour reproductions of paintings by community members accompanied by extracts from their dialogues. Short extracts also appear in Berryman, op. cit. For a selection of Ernesto Cardenal's poetry see his *Psalms*, Sheed and Ward 1981. The information pack *Nicaragua: Church and Revolution*, produced by the Catholic Institute for International Relations, 1984, contains many important documents including copies of letters from the Pope and the Nicaraguan bishops, and the FSLN policy statement on religion.

On the revolution in general a good lively introduction is George Black, *Triumph of the People*, Zed Press 1981. Thomas Walker, *Nicaragua: the Land of Sandino*, Westview Press 1981, is another good account. 'Rius', *Nicaragua for Beginners*, Unwin 1986, is a good factual introduction presented in comic – book style. For a very useful and reasonably objective assessment of developments since the revolution see Dianna Melrose, *Nicaragua – The Threat of a Good Example?*, Oxfam 1985. CIIR's *Nicaragua* in their Comment series of booklets is a good short introduction. Harris and Vilas, op. cit., is a collection of analytical essays on various themes including the economy, the Miskitos, the workers' movement, religion, and US involvement. The almost identically named *Nicaragua: Revolution Under Siege*, Bookmarks 1985, by Mike Gonzalez, is a socialist critique of the revolution. Shirley Christian, *Nicaragua: Revolution in the Family*, Random House 1985, is critical from a different political perspective. Dale Kietzman (ed.) *Into the Crossfire*, Marshalls 1985, is a very theologically and politically conservative impression of events in Central America including Nicaragua. For a journalist's observations of life in Nicaragua see Peter Stalker's 22-page report 'A Journey through the New Nicaragua', *New Internationalist*, February 1986. *Nicaragua Libre!*, Nicaragua Solidarity Campaign 1985, is a collection of impressions compiled by forty-one visitors from Britain. Gordon White and Kate Young (eds.), *Nicaragua after the Revolution: Problems and Prospects*, IDS Publications, University of Sussex 1985, contains four essays on the economy, agrarian reform, and the position of women. For specific issues see, on Somoza, Bernard Diederich, *Somoza*, Junction Books 1982; on Sandino, Gregorio Selser, *Sandino*, Monthly Review Press 1981; on women in the revolution, Jane Deighton, Rossana Horsley, Sarah Stewart and Cathy Cain, *Sweet Ramparts: Women in Revolutionary Nicaragua*, War on Want/Nicaragua Solidarity Campaign 1983; on human rights, *Nicaragua: The Human Rights Record*, Amnesty International Publications 1986; on the effect of the *contra* attacks, Teófilo Cabestrero, *Blood of the Innocent: Victims of the Contras' War in Nicaragua*, Orbis/CIIR 1985, and Yvonne Dilling (ed.), *What We Have Seen And Heard: The Effects of the Contra War Against Nicaragua*, Witness for Peace 1985; on the impact of the revolution on agriculture, Joseph Collins, *What Difference Could a Revolution Make?*, Food First 1982; on US involvement, Jenny Pearce, *Under the Eagle: US Intervention in Central America and the Caribbean*, Latin America Bureau 1982, and Marlene Dixon (ed.) *On Trial: Reagan's War Against Nicaragua*, Zed Books 1985.

Bruce Marcus has brought together some important speeches and statements by Sandinista leaders in *Sandinistas Speak*, Pathfinder Press 1982, and *Nicaragua: the Sandinista People's Revolution*, Pathfinder Press 1985. A useful collection of interviews with government officials and others appears in Zwerling and Martin, op.

cit.; some of the items are rather short, but the inclusion of interviews with prominent opponents of the Sandinistas, including a senior church official, newspaper editor, and *contra* leaders, enhances the book's value. For further interviews with the counterrevolutionaries see Dieter Eich and Carlos Rincon (eds.), *The Contras: Interviews with Anti-Sandinistas*, Synthesis 1986. A book which examines the *contras* from the inside is Christopher Dickey, *With the Contras: A Reporter in the Wilds of Nicaragua*, Faber 1986. Frances Moore Lappé and Joseph Collins record the (occasionally critical) views of some 'ordinary' Nicaraguans on the revolution in *Now We Can Speak*, Food First 1982. Omar Cabezas, *Fire from the Mountain*, Jonathan Cape 1985, is one participant's first-hand account of the revolution. A novel which captures the atmosphere of Nicaragua in the pre-revolutionary years is *To Bury Our Fathers: A Novel of Nicaragua*, Readers International 1985, written in exile by the present vice-president of the country Sergio Ramírez. A selection of the work of Roger Sanchez, resident cartoonist with the Sandinista newspaper *Barricada*, is available in *I'm Only Doing This to Help You Calm Down*, Nicaragua Solidarity Campaign 1986. Salman Rushdie discusses his visit to Nicaragua in mid-1986, the role of religion in the country and his impressions of, among others, Ernesto Cardenal, Miguel D'Escoto and Uriel Molina in *The Jaguar Smile: A Nicaraguan Journey*, Pan Books 1987.

Notes

1. The Church in Latin America: From an Alliance with Power to an Option for the Poor

1. José Míguez Bonino, *Doing Theology in a Revolutionary Situation*, SPCK and Fortress Press 1975, p. 6.

2. This term is used throughout because its rough English equivalent 'consciousness-raising' has a more individualist connotation and does not quite capture the idea of a collective development of political awareness implied by the Spanish term.

3. Gustavo Gutiérrez, *A Theology of Liberation*, Orbis Books 1973 and SCM Press 1974, p. 276. This is widely regarded as the seminal work of liberation theology.

4. Hugo Assmann, *Practical Theology of Liberation*, Search Press 1975, p. 139.

2. The Church Militant

1. Ernesto Cardenal, *The Gospel in Solentiname*, four vols., Orbis Books 1976–82.

2. *Sojourners* (Washington DC), March 1983, p. 22.

3. Fernando Cardenal, 'Como cristiano revolucionario encontré un nuevo camino', *Nicarauac*, 2nd year, no. 5 (April-June 1981) pp. 99–108, quoted in Philip Berryman, *The Religious Roots of Rebellion*, Orbis Books and SCM Press 1984, p. 64; see also Téofilo Cabastrero, *Ministers of God, Ministers of the People*, Orbis Books and Zed Press 1983, p. 83.

4. Fernando Cardenal, 'A Letter to My Friends', p. 9; see also Cabastrero, op. cit., p. 60.

5. Ernesto Cardenal, *The Gospel in Solentiname*, vol. 4, pp. 51–52, quoted in Berryman, op. cit., p. 18.

6. Luis Serra, 'Ideology, Religion and the Class Struggle in the Nicaraguan Revolution', *Nicaragua: A Revolution under Siege*, ed. Richard Harris and Carlos M. Vilas, Zed Books 1985, p. 166.

7. Cabestrero, op. cit., p. 112–13.

8. Ibid., pp. 76–7; cf. p. 82.

9. José Míguez Bonino, *Christians and Marxists: The Mutual Challenge to Revolution*, Hodder & Stoughton 1976, p. 40. Professor Míguez Bonino, an Argentinian Methodist, is one of the few leading theologians of liberation outside the Catholic communion.

10. Cabestrero, op. cit., p. 77.

11. Míguez Bonino, op. cit., p. 16.

12. Penny Lernoux, *Cry of the People*, Penguin Books 1982, p. 102.

13. Cabestrero, op. cit., p. 60.   14. Ibid., p. 27.

15. 'Continent of Violence', *Between Honesty and Hope: Documents from and about the Church in Latin America, Issued at Lima by the Peruvian Bishops' Commission for Social Action*, Maryknoll Publications 1970, p. 84, quoted in Gustavo Gutierrez, *A Theology of Liberation*, Orbis Books 1973 and SCM Press 1974, pp. 108–9 (emphasis theirs).

16. Cabestrero, op. cit. p.74.

17. Pilar Arias (ed.), *Nicaragua: Revolucion – Relatos de combatientes del Frente Sandinista*, Siglo XXI, Mexico City 1980; quoted in Berryman, op. cit., p. 80.

18. It is not clear whether Obando actually refused the car or accepted it and then sold it; nevertheless it was important as a symbolic act.

19. José Manuel Ruiz, 'Los obispos nicaragüenses frente al somocismo', *El Nuevo Diario* (Managua), 3 March 1984, p. 2.

20. Daniel H. Levine, *Religion and Politics in Latin America*, Princeton University Press 1981, pp. 54–5 & 297.

3. By Schisms Rent Asunder

1. This is discussed further in Chapter 4.

2. *Contra* is the term used widely in Nicaragua, the United States and elsewhere to describe the armed forces opposed to the Nicaraguan government. It is a contraction of the Spanish term for counter-revolutionaries, *contra-revolucionarios*.

3. Though the bishops have maintained a belief that the *contras* are Nicaraguans, and this has been offered as an explanation for their apparent refusal to condemn them – the church is for all citizens of the country.

4. Miguel D'Escoto, 'The Church Born of the People in Nicaragua', *Revolution in Central America*, ed. Stanford Central America Action Network, Westview Press, Boulder Colorado 1983, pp. 375–6.

5. Teófilo Cabestrero, *Ministers of God, Ministers of the People*, Orbis Books and Zed Press 1983, p. 65.

6. 'Commentary on the Pastoral Letter of the Bishops of Nicaragua', *Carta del CAV* (Managua), No. 2., April 1984.

7. Fernando Cardenal, 'A Letter to my Friends', p. 3.

8. *National Catholic Reporter*, 20 July 1984, p. 8.

9. *The Tablet*, 26 April 1986, p. 440; *The Tablet*, 23 March 1985, p. 309.

10. Humberto Belli, 'The Church in Nicaragua: Under Attack From Within and Without', *Religion in Communist Lands*, Vol. 12, No. 1, Spring 1984, pp. 45–6.

11. Luis Serra, 'Ideology, Religion and the Class Struggle in the Nicaraguan Revolution', *Nicaragua: A Revolution under Siege*, ed. Richard Harris and Carlos M. Vilas, Zed Books 1985, p. 171.

12. Bruce Marcus (ed.), *Nicaragua: the Sandinista People's Revolution*, Pathfinder Press, New York 1985, p. 286.

13. Ibid., p. 14.   14. Ibid., p. 38.

15. 'Testimony', *Carta del CAV*, No. 2, April 1984.

16. Cabestrero, op. cit., p. 74.

17. Cardenal, 'A Letter to My Friends', p. 11; Cabestrero, op. cit., p. 69.

18. Cardenal, 'A Letter to my Friends', p. 11.

19. Cabestrero, op. cit., p. 124.

20. 'La Crisis del Catolicismo Nicaragüense: Perspectivas Sociológicas sobre el Problema', *Amanecer* (Managua), January 1985, an interview with François Houtart by José Argüello.

21. 'Reto de la evangelización en una sociedad revolucionaria', *El Nuevo Diario*, 31 January 1984, p. 2.

22. Pax Christi International, *Nicaragua – Human Rights Reports 2*, Omega Books, Antwerp 1981, p. 104.

23. Serra, loc. cit., p. 158.

24. César Jerez, *The Church and the Nicaraguan Revolution*, CIIR Justice Papers No. 5, 1984, p. 15.

25. J. W. Meyer, 'Passing through the Fire', *Into the Crossfire*, ed. Dale Kietzman, Marshall 1985, p. 47. See also below, p. 57.

26. 'La Crisis del Catolicismo Nicaragüense'.

27. Jane Deighton, Rosanna Horsley, Sarah Stewart and Cathy Cain, *Sweet Ramparts: Women in Revolutionary Nicaragua*, War on Want and Nicaragua Solidarity Campaign 1983, p. 147.

28. D'Escoto, loc. cit., p. 375.

4. A State of Tension

1. *Nicaragua: The Human Rights Record*, Amnesty International Publications 1986, p. 21.

2. Ibid., pp. 30f.; pp. 10f.   3. Ibid., p. 21.

4. Quoted in Luis Serra, 'Ideology, Religion and the Class Struggle in the Nicaraguan Revolution', *Nicaragua: A Revolution under Siege*, ed. Richard Harris and Carlos M. Vilas, Zed Books 1985, p. 162.

5. César Jerez, *The Church and the Nicaraguan Revolution*, CIIR Justice Papers No. 5., 1984, pp. 15f.

6. J. W. Meyer, 'Passing through the Fire', *Into the Crossfire*, ed. Dale Kietzman, Marshall 1985, pp. 47–8.

7. Fernando Cardenal, 'Como cristiano revolucionario encontré un nuevo camino', *Nicarauac*, p. 103, quoted in Philip Berryman, *The Religious Roots of Rebellion*, Orbis Books and SCM Press 1984, p. 64; also quoted in Fernando Cardenal, 'A Letter to my Friends', p. 9.

5. Political Priests and a Polish Pope

1. Teófilo Cabestrero, *Ministers of God, Ministers of the People*, Orbis Books and Zed Press 1983, p. 78.
2. Ibid., p. 130.   3. Ibid., p. 4.
4. *Origins*, 17 March 1983, Vol. 12, No. 40, p. 635.
5. Liberation theology has been the subject of two recent statements by the Vatican's Congregation for the Doctrine of the Faith: 'Instruction on Certain Aspects of the "Theology of Liberation"' (1984), and 'Instruction on Christian Freedom and Liberation' (1986).
6. Both Fernando and Ernesto Cardenal refer to this exception: see Cabestrero, op. cit., p. 67, and *Playboy*, September 1983, p. 140.
7. *The Tablet*, 9 February 1985, p. 139.
8. *The Guardian*, 5 July 1986.
9. Opening address to three-day conference of the Roman Curia and the Brazilian bishops, March 1986, *The Tablet*, 22 March 1986, p. 322.
10. *Playboy*, September 1983, p. 140.   11. Ibid.
12. Charles Antoine, 'Nicaragua: In the Footsteps of the Polish Church?', *Religion in Communist Lands*, Vol. 12, No. 3, Winter 1984, pp. 276–8.
13. *The Tablet*, 2 March 1985, p. 224.

6. A Better Mañana?

1. Quoted in José Míguez Bonino, *Christians and Marxists: the Mutual Challenge to Revolution*, Hodder & Stoughton 1976, p. 27.
2. *The Tablet*, 15 March 1986, p. 296.
3. Dianna Melrose makes the interesting point that Nicaragua is estimated to be facing about 15,000 counter-revolutionaries which, proportionately, 'would be equivalent to Britain facing attack and sabotage from more than a quarter of a million terrorists'. Dianna Melrose, *Nicaragua: The Threat of a Good Example?*, Oxfam 1985, p. 29 and p. 63 n. 3.
4. The American bishops have also been strongly critical of some aspects of Sandinista government policy – for example on the question of human rights and the treatment of Bishop Vega and Mgr Carballo.
5. *The Tablet*, 4 October 1986, pp. 1058–59.
6. *The Independent*, 25 November 1986; *The Tablet* 29 November 1986, p. 1296.

Index

education, 3, 8, 12, 43, 53–4, 57, 66
El Salvador, 12, 75, 76
Evangelicals, 11, 16, 41

FAO, 26
Fonseca, Carlos, 21, 38
FSLN, 18, 23, 25, 38; and the
revolution, vii, 11, 17, 23; Christians and, 15–24, 37, 45, 57–8;
and Marxism, 17, 20–21, 36, 49,
54, 56, 57, 65, 68, 69; relations
with the church, 17, 21, 26, 27,
30, 31, 32, 34, 38, 42, 45, chapter
4 (48–58) passim, 61, 71, 74–5;
and the people, 23, 33, 40, 73;
commando raids, 26; and religion, 16, 31, 38, 40, 42, 45,
56–58, 77; and Miskito relocation, 31, 52–53; and Pope's visit,
66, 67

García, Gaspar, 19, 21, 22, 56
Gaudium et Spes, 5
Giglio, Paolo, 74
Guatemala, 75, 76
Gutiérrez, Gustavo, 7, 20, 80

Honduras, 36, 52, 74
Houtart, François, 41, 45, 46
human rights, 17, 23, 52–53, 78, 83

Iglesia, 50, 54

Jara, José de la, 15
Jerez, César, 44, 56, 76
Jesuits, 17, 23, 59, 60, 62, 65
Jesus Christ, 14, 18, 19, 30, 39, 41,
72

Kingdom of God, 7, 14, 19, 30, 72

Lang, Edgard, 38
La Prensa, 23, 49
Las Casas, Bartolomé de, 2

Levine, Daniel, 28
Lezcano, José, 12
Liberation Theology, vii, 20, 27, 36,
41; origin of, 7; and Marxism, 7,
64; influence of, 8, 16, 43, 64–5;
FSLN and, 45, 57; the US and,
56; the Vatican and, 63, 64–65,
66, 75, 83
Literacy Crusade, 30, 31, 33, 54, 60
Los Doce (The Twelve), 18
L'Osservatore Romano, 72

Marx/Marxism, 6, 7, 56, 73;
Christianity and, vii, 20–21, 37;
and Liberation Theology, 7, 64;
and FSLN, 17, 20–21, 36, 49,
54, 56, 57, 65, 68, 69; priests and,
20–21, 57; and 'popular church',
32, 37; the Pope and, 65, 68, 69
Maryknoll Community, 15, 59, 69
Medellín (Latin American Bishops'
Conference 1968), 7, 8, 9, 16, 22,
24, 28, 43, 60
Mexico, 36, 74
Míguez Bonino, José, 2, 20, 21,
80–81
Miskito Indians, 31, 52–53, 78
Molina, Uriel, 15, 50, 79
Monimbó, 23

National Catholic Reporter, 36
National Guard, 15, 16, 22, 23, 24,
25, 36, 53, 63
New York Times, 36

Obando y Bravo, Miguel, 24–26,
30, 36, 44, 49, 55–57, 68–69,
71–72, 74, 81
OPEN 3 community, 15
Ortega, Daniel, 21, 49, 55, 74, 75

Panama, 49, 74
Parrales, Edgar, 20, 35, 37, 57,
59–65, 69, 71, 77